The Best Shooting in Scotland

Cape Wrath

John O'Groats

Thurso

Wick

CAITHNESS

Lewis

Stornoway

SUTHERLAND

The Highlands

ROSS-SHIRE

Fraserburgh

Elgin

Buckie

Banff

Harris

Nairn

Peterhead

North Uist

Inverness

MORAYSHIRE

Skye

Grantown-on-Spey

Speyside

ABERDEENSHIRE

INVERNESS-SHIRE

South Uist

Loch Ness

Monadhliath Mts.

The Cairngorms

Deeside

Aberdeen

Rum

Glen More

Banchory

Eigg

Braemar

Ballater

Grampian Mts.

Fort William

Loch Rannoch

The Angus Glens

Coll

Kirriemuir

Montrose

Loch Tay

Tay

Strathmore

Forfar

Tiree

Mull

Aberfeldy

Dundee

Arbroath

Oban

PERTHSHIRE

Firth of Tay

Crieff

Perth

St. Andrews

ARGYLL

STIRLINGS.

FIFE

Jura

Loch Lomond

Firth of Forth

DUNBARTONSHIRE

EAST LOTHIAN

Islay

Edinburgh

Berwick-upon-Tweed

The Lammermuirs

Glasgow

Arran

RENFREWS.

Peebles

Tweedale

KINTYRE

Ayr

AYRSHIRE

The Borders

Cheviot Hills

Mull of Kintyre

DUMFRIESSHIRE

0   25 miles

0   40 km.

GALLOWAY

Dumfries

Annan

WIGTOWNSHIRE

Carlisle

Stranraer

Wigtown

THE
BEST
SHOOTING
IN SCOTLAND

JOHN ANDREWS

LOCHAR PUBLISHING • MOFFAT • SCOTLAND

Published by Lochar Publishing Ltd
MOFFAT DG10 9ED

British Library Cataloguing in Publication Data
Andrews, John
  The best shooting in Scotland.
  1. Scotland. Game animals. Shooting
  I. Title
  799.21309411

ISBN 0-948403-33-0

Typeset in Plantin on 10/11pt by Chapterhouse,
The Cloisters, Formby, L37 3PX

Printed in Great Britain by BPCC Wheatons Ltd, Exeter

Map by David Langworth
Jacket photograph by Joyce Salazar

for Joyce, my lady

Contents

Introduction

Perhaps those of us in Scotland who are keen shooting people do ourselves a disservice by broadcasting the fact that there is such quality and quantity of sport available here for the gameshooter. But the Scots have always been a hospitable people and sporting visitors may be assured of receiving a traditional warm welcome. It is not in the Scottish nature to be selfish about our sport. We are proud of it and happy to share our enjoyment of this superb natural heritage. In return for this sharing we do ask that our long-established sporting codes and traditions are respected and that our high standards of sportsmanship are observed and practised by our guests.

We have an abundance of game in Scotland because the basic ingredient – suitable habitat and environment – has been skilfully husbanded over the years, and the stocks of wild game carefully preserved and managed in order to produce an annual harvest of the shootable surplus. In these days of commercialised shooting there is sometimes pressure on those responsible for game management to overstretch the resource. There may be a temptation to squeeze a little more out of what would be a sensible cull of a wild stock of game and to release rather more reared birds than an area can sustain without detriment to the health of the birds or damage to the environment.

It is hoped that visitors will not encourage any such malpractice by making demands for excessive bags. Any fool can gun down a pile of half-grown pheasants lumbering past at head height. There is no merit in this for anyone. Sporting shooting should never be a numbers game. The true satisfaction of the sport comes from full participation in the total experience, and exercising the skill involved in dealing with testing and well-presented birds.

This book is intended as a reference for the reader who is unfamiliar with Scotland, its heritage of wild game and long tradition of sporting shooting. It provides a detailed picture of the natural history and practical husbandry of each game species, an account of how each form of the sport is carried out, and an insight into the attitudes and way of life of the people who are involved in its management and operation.

Each section is followed by details of where the best of that particular type of sport is provided and to whom enquiries should be addressed. Top quality shooting, where the bag is numbered in hundreds, is naturally expensive as, inevitably, it takes a substantial and costly infrastructure to produce. The shooter of average means should not be deterred by this. A large bag of game is not necessarily essential for a good day out with the gun. There are many facets to an enjoyable sporting occasion – the sheer beauty of hill and woodland, the clear invigorating air of a crisp autumn morn, the company of like-minded friends, the joy of watching good dogs at work, the camaraderie and teamwork between guns, keepers, pickers-up and beaters, plus the satisfaction of the occasional superb shot. Such ingredients make a day to savour and remember.

There are numerous opportunities to be had for occasions like this, which offer the visitor a delightful taste of the total Scottish sporting experience where the size of the bag is not the major concern and the costs are not prohibitive. For many visitors this is often where they may find their personal choice of the very best of sporting shooting in Scotland.

It is my hope that this book will help you to discover such an experience.

Ceud mìle fàilte.

COCK PTARMIGAN in summer plumage. (*Sport in Scotland*)

RANNOCH MOOR, an inhospitable landscape but home to many hundreds of red deer. (*Perthshire Tourist Board*)

1 The Gameshooter's Scotland

THE START OF IT ALL

THE BEST GAMESHOOTING and deerstalking facilities in Europe have long been found in Scotland. Historically, this small colourful nation has drawn sporting visitors across its border since shooting game and stalking deer came to be a leisure pursuit rather than just a means of acquiring meat for the table.

The sport has long had royal support and promotion which continues to this day. Queen Victoria was probably the most effective public relations agent that Scotland has ever had. She loved this land and was particularly fond of the romantic image of the Highlands. Although she disdained to take an active part in sport, her beloved Albert was delighted to indulge himself in the cornucopia of sporting goodies that was spread before him. His opportune marriage had availed him of much but probably his most highly valued treasure was the access which it gave him to the finest shooting and stalking in the land. He made good use of this bounty, becoming a most enthusiastic shooter of game and stalker of deer. Perhaps he became a little over enthusiastic. Once, when a guest of the Duke of Atholl at Blair Castle, he spied two stags on the lawn outside his bedroom window. Seizing his rifle, he quickly indulged in a royal execution, doubtless proud of notching up two kills before breakfast whilst still attired in his nightshirt!

His spouse, Queen Victoria, was the original 'white settler'. When she bought the Balmoral estate and began to spend a great deal of her time there she set a trend that top-drawer society of the day rushed to emulate.

The expansion of a highly efficient railway system meant that sporting people could now leave Euston and be conveyed north in sumptuous comfort, and be downing grouse on the Perthshire moors some 16 short hours later. The son and heir of Victoria, Edward, Prince of Wales, had plenty of free time on his hands during the many long years of his mother's reign, and he loved nothing better than to spend this time in shooting. Like his mother he was very fond of Scotland, particularly Deeside and Speyside, and his enthusiasm gave the royal seal of approval to Scottish sport, adding an extra incentive to the growing hordes of tweed-clad southern sporting persons who packed the northbound trains on 11 August.

A Highland estate became the fashionable thing to have, and the threadbare sporran of many an impecunious Highland laird grew heavy with English gold as many of Scotland's bens and glens were acquired by new absentee landlords.

Sporting tourism was underway and it was not long before whole rural economies became dependent on the pursuit of grouse and deer, establishing a new form of land use which flourishes to this day. The ranks of Sassenach sportsmen are now swelled by visitors from many parts of the globe who come to enjoy sport of an unrivalled quality and quantity in a unique land of beauty, history and romance. Scotland offers a sporting experience that would be difficult to match anywhere else in the world.

THE COUNTRY AND ITS GAME

In order to see why Scotland is a country so hospitable to wildlife and game it is necessary only to look at a map. It will be noted that there is a relatively sparse network of roads, few large towns, a high proportion of the overall area is comprised of uplands, and a great deal of open green space exists. The total population barely exceeds 5 million which is about the same as the whole of London. Therefore the right ecosystem exists with adequate diverse habitat to support a wide variety of game species. To appreciate fully why some areas provide better sport than others and why some species should thrive in particular areas, it is necessary to examine in some detail the topography, habitat, climate and land use of the differing parts of Scotland.

There is an extensive coastline which on the

SCONE PALACE, home of the Earl of Mansfield and the centre of an estate with all types of quality shooting. (*Perthshire Tourist Board*)

west is inclined to be mainly rocky with many offshore islands when north of Glasgow. On the east there is more of a coastal plain which is intersected with a number of long and wide river estuaries, notably the Firths of Forth, Tay and Moray. To the west there is the Solway Firth, on the border with England, and the Firth of Clyde into which drain the waters of Loch Lomond via the river Leven. These firths and estuaries are important wintering grounds for wildfowl. Within their shallow sheltered waters and on their sand and mud banks, they provide strategic night roosting areas for the many thousands of greylag and pinkfooted geese that migrate to Scotland every autumn and winter from their principal breeding grounds in Iceland and Greenland. All these estuaries, with the possible exception of the Firth of Clyde, hold a permanent population of geese throughout the winter, with numbers fluctuating somewhat but invariably attracting a considerable number of night roosting residents. These estuaries have been created by major river systems which flow through rich and flat arable land. These are conditions which suit the requirements of the migrant geese, which are inclined to fly out from the estuary roosts at first light to feed by day in the fertile farmlands which adjoin the estuaries and line the course of the rivers which enter them.

The large estuaries also provide both night feeding grounds and undisturbed daytime roosts for the host of migrant duck which spend their winters in Scotland. Most species of duck, both migrant and locally bred, are to be found on the estuaries at some time or

other during the winter. In particular these areas attract much of the inland population when harsh winter conditions petrify many of the freshwater ponds and marshes, forcing the fowl to seek an easier living in the slightly softer conditions at the coast. The widgeon is the coastal duckshooter's principal quarry and one of this duck's most favoured areas is the Dornoch Firth, which the widgeon flocks visit in multitudes. These estuaries and firths are the areas where 'real wildfowling' takes place and the potential fowler has probably the greatest scope in the Tay estuary and the Moray and Dornoch Firths.

Moving inland for a further look at the overall distribution of the various game species in Scotland, if we start at the Border country, which is largely highish ground of rolling grass hill with heather moorland on areas of greater altitude, it will be clear that this provides a habitat suitable only for upland game. There is little in the way of deciduous woodland here and most of the trees are inclined to be foreigners, including some vast blocks of the unpleasant, controversial but highly commercial Sitka spruce. These are, for the greater part, sterile deserts for most types of game but form an ideal refuge for foxes, crows and other enemies of the game producer. Gamekeepers, whose land adjoins these areas, often have a nightmare task in attempting to control the constant stream of game-gobbling predators that issue forth from these havens. These vast blocks of woodland do provide some cover for both roe and red deer, but that is about the limit of their sporting potential.

Just inside the border, to the north of the

Solway Firth, is the delightful and often overlooked region of Dumfries and Galloway. To the north of Gatehouse of Fleet and Newton Stewart is a very attractive area where commercial forestry has been dealt with rather more sympathetically than normal. Some of the blocks of spruce have been split up and more open ground than usual has been left. This is an area which supports a good healthy stock of red deer as well as roe, and some very fine specimens are to be found here.

From the centre of the Border country and spreading eastwards is an upland area of largely open heather hill, managed for sheep and grouse production. Some very fine grouse moors are to be found here among the Tweedsmuir, Moorfoot, Lammermuir and Pentland Hills. The coastal plain from Berwick-on-Tweed round to the fringes of Edinburgh is largely arable land and, in addition to some good pheasant shoots, is a particularly favourable area for partridge with its mixed cropping and relatively light rainfall. Over to the west, pastoral Ayrshire has some notable pheasant and low-ground shooting, with a few good grouse moors to the east of the district.

The central belt of Scotland is its industrial heartland, the unattractive country between Glasgow and Edinburgh containing little game but supporting an incredible population of magpies, crows and foxes. Curiously, one is far more likely to see a fox in this heavily populated area than in any of the more remote parts of the country. These urbanised foxes live an almost jackal-like existence, raiding dustbins and dining on the occasional cat.

Both major Scottish cities are fortunate in that, immediately to the north, particularly in the case of Glasgow, lies some very attractive countryside. It is even possible to shoot game and wildfowl within the boundary of the city of Glasgow. To the west of this striving cultural capital of Europe lies Dunbartonshire which contains the superb Loch Lomond, a favoured winter roost for greylag geese. Rather unusually, Lomond's attractive islands have long supported a substantial herd of truly wild fallow deer. These beasts, some of which are pure white, are, like the yew trees on the isle of Inch Lonaig, reputed to have been introduced on the command of the nation's favourite king – Robert the Bruce. In addition to the unusual sight of fallow deer grazing on the shores of Lomond's islands or even swimming between them, it is also possible to see the magnificent capercaillie as they occasionally fly from island to island. A small colony of these large members of the grouse family frequents the many stands of native Caledonian pine to be found on several of the islands.

Between Glasgow and Stirling lies little to interest the gameshooter, although the traveller might care to give a passing glance to the field of Bannockburn where the Bruce had his most celebrated home win. North of Stirling one begins to enter God's own country for the field sportsman.

Perthshire or, as local government bureaucracy would now have it, Perth and Kinross District (how unevocative), has it all. Not for nothing have the landed gentry established many large estates in the straths of the Earn and Tay. These aristocratic land-owners occupy most of this favoured area, tenaciously clinging on to and defending against all-comers this desirable land which their ancestors fought over, stole and plundered. In general their husbandry over the centuries has been good and most of the estates as well as being efficiently and productively farmed have also been managed for optimum game production. This is one of the main reasons why there is such an attractive landscape in Perthshire of mixed woodland and arable, providing the finest of habitat for low-ground game and other desirable wildlife – readily seen here in abundance.

As well as providing ideal board and lodging for low-ground game, the fat farmlands of Perthshire supply a winter larder for many thousands of grey geese. Nearby Loch Leven, which is actually in Kinross, is a popular roost, particularly for pinkfeet. The dawn exodus of vast squadrons of these great birds from Leven and the Tay estuary out over the Perthshire fields is one of the most stirring sights a sportsman could behold. It is not so many years since the sight of hordes of grey geese decending on arable fields turned many a Perthshire farmer quite purple with rage. He hated to think that these birds might be feeding off him for nothing. The local gunners benefited by this situation as 20 years ago it was possible to get gooseshooting simply for the asking and some farmers even supplied the cartridges. Geese inflict some damage on winter sown cereals and they do feed heavily on the 'early bite', the first new grass of the

THE LADY seems impressed. Cock and hen pheasant in spring. (*John Andrews*)

season. But certainly no farmer has ever been bankrupted by them and these days the birds may actually produce a revenue for the landowner for no outlay whatsoever – a very fine situation which has much appeal for many farmers. Gone are the days when the local lads could have free gooseshooting. Now Scotland hosts another migration in addition to the geese. Up from the south every winter comes a growing horde of sportsmen, many of these crossing the English Channel, all lured to the chase of the wild goose and willing to pay handsomely for the privilege.

To the north and west of Perthshire the land changes abruptly in character. At Crieff in the west and Blairgowrie in the east the lowland fields of grain begin to merge into the steeper ground of heather upland and craggy hill. Here rise the foothills of the Grampians, the start of grouse and red deer territory, and there are many famous estates in these areas where their pursuit is paramount. Much of this grouse and deer ground is also occupied by the Scottish or mountain hare, particularly in the area between Loch Earn and Loch Tay where incredible numbers of these creatures may be seen when they adopt their snow-white coats of winter.

To the north-east of Edinburgh lies the 'Kingdom' of Fife, home of coalmines, intensive agriculture, picturesque fishing ports and golf. There are some excellent pheasant shoots in Fife and good mixed low-ground shooting. The 'Kingdom' is also the principal area in Scotland for foxhunting – the real thing, red coats, horns, hounds and all that.

Up country across the silvery Tay, so beloved by Scotland's best bad poet, William McGonagall, lies the district and former county of Angus. Very similar to Perthshire in many ways, Angus is not quite so up-market as there is not such a monopoly of the patrician-owned estates. The lower ground between Kirriemuir and Brechin is the start of the Howe of the Mearns, Lewis Grassic Gibbon country. Here are to be found many small owner-occupied mixed farms worked by a dying breed of countryman, the independent Angus farmer. Great characters these, a kindly hospitable breed who, generously, may still give permission for a walk across their ground to the local and visiting sportsman. The spell-binding glens of Angus – Isla, Esk, Prosen and Clova – provide an unbeatable setting for the excellent grouse shooting which the area provides. Above the glens, in the foothills and stretching far into the Grampian mountains, is renowned red deer country. This is an area where grouse and deer overlap and stags may often be found descending to the lower grouse moors.

The whole of the Grampian mountains, north to the Cairngorms and Speyside and east towards Banff and Aberdeen provide good grouse moors on the lower slopes and support healthy stocks of red deer on the higher ground. This central and eastern area provides a better habitat for game than the wetter areas towards the west coast. The ground to the east is inclined to be less acidic and drier than the west. This produces more nutritious heather and a climate more conducive to grouse production, factors which also suit the red deer herds.

To the east the Grampians are drained by the rivers Dee and Don. These river valleys provide a wide variety of low-ground game and some excellent mixed shooting is to be found there. To the north is the spacious strath of the river Spey, a truly magical area of birch woods, heather, great stands of superb Scots pine, marshes and mixed arable. Speyside provides every possible form of gameshooting that could be desired. It contains some of the finest grouse moors in the country, it is roe deer country *par excellence*, and the area holds an enormous population producing a high number of medal-class heads every season. For the sportsman who desires a good mixed day in breathtaking surroundings, Speyside is paradise. Grouse, pheasant, blackgame, partridge, wildfowl, pigeon and ground game may all feature in a day's bag on some estates. Red deer on Speyside do not confine themselves to the high hill, many occupying the lower woodlands, and it is possible to come across them almost anywhere.

There is a great mass of low ground in the north east, extending round the base of the Grampians from Stonehaven, past Aberdeen, way across the broad green lands of Buchan with its attractive coastal towns of Banff, MacDuff, Portsoy, Buckie, Lossiemouth and Nairn. It sweeps round past the foothills of the Monadliath Mountains to Inverness, the unofficial capital of the Highlands. This ground is fairly rich and fertile with arable and beef production being the main agricultural interest. It is all good mixed game country with a healthy population of wild game and some excellent driven pheasant shoots. On the higher ground there are some great grouse holding areas as, although the area is subject to cold winters with biting north east winds, the birds benefit from the relatively dry conditions which are inclined to prevail in spring.

To the west of the Great Glen which runs diagonally across Scotland from Fort William in the west to Inverness in the east is a barren mountainous area intersected by glens and also by sea lochs on the west coast. Certain areas contain reasonable numbers of red deer, but grouse and other game are not found in any quantity.

North of Inverness one is deep into the Highlands. This is the country of the Gael. In many rural areas the local people still prefer to use Gaelic as their everyday tongue and the area is rich in Celtic mythology and stories of the warring clans. The mountainous area extends up the western and central part of the country to the north coast of Sutherland. Apart from ptarmigan on the highest tops and a sparse stock of grouse, the main game species is the red deer which is found in small herds throughout the area. Here the deer are inclined to be a little smaller and lighter than in more favourable areas, and the stags do not generally produce anything spectacular in the way of antler growth. But the deerstalker in this area has adequate compensation as there can be few more spectacular locations in which to pursue the sport.

The east coast north of Inverness is a different type of terrain, flatter, more fertile and drier, providing reasonable conditions for low-ground game. Although not present in large quantities, a pleasing variety of game

may be found right up the east coast to John O'Groats. On many of the farms in this area the wild grey partridge flourishes as the light sandy soil and drier climate suits it well. Much of the coastline is formed by steep cliffs containing many caves and these are home to the rock dove – a real test of shotgunning skill when attempting to shoot them from a boat at sea.

The furthest north eastern corner of

Scotland is a different land altogether. The character of Caithness is unlike the rest of the Highlands, more Norse than Gaelic, and it betrays much of the influence of past invaders in its place names. It is a curious, flat and at first sight dull country, but it has very much a fascination of its own. One of its most obvious characteristics is the use of slate flagstones from local quarries to act as field boundaries. There are virtually no trees in Caithness and

OADING UP the bag.
(*John Andrews*)

the raw material for fence posts would be hard to come by.

The treasures of Caithness are not immediately apparent, but the more time that is spent there the more it is possible to discover its many delights. Its grouse shooting is not the stuff of big driven days but it has many pleasant moors that are ideal for dogging. Its vast flat expanses of heather with moderate stocks of grouse are also eminently suitable for falconry and there are several places where this evocative mediaeval field-sport is practised.

The lands of Caithness are not totally monopolised by big estates and there are many owner-occupied working farms with large acreages where roughshooting may still be had for the asking. Many of these farms, particularly those along the east coast, provide a suitable habitat for a surprising variety of wild game. Most have a few modest arable fields growing oats, barley and turnips, which often slope up to moorland of mediocre ill-managed heather and rough hill grasses. The lower ground will often hide a surprising number of small wild hill pheasants, good coveys of partridge, lots of snipe, sometimes lots of woodcock, also hares and rabbits, and where there is marshland or ponds there may be plenty of mallard. Greylag geese may frequent these farms for short periods on their migration south, and woodpigeon stocks fluctuate according to available food. Farms near the coast may provide an interesting diversion if rock doves are found to be feeding on oat or barley stubble. The doves may be decoyed in the same fashion as woodpigeon

and as they are generally more erratic and swifter in flight than the woodies they provide challenging shooting.

These wide open moorlands of Caithness do contain some rather good quality red deer. Because of the nature of the ground, stalking these may be a long drawn out affair as the beasts are often in the position of being able to see for miles and are extremely difficult to approach, and this has given rise to a very unusual form of deerstalking which is seldom practised elsewhere. As the roe lie up at times in the thick reed beds they may be flushed from their lies like hares and a carefully placed rifle bullet will bowl them over in mid flight. Perhaps this style of 'jump-shooting' is a bit too 'cowboyish' for some tastes but it is an extremely effective means of putting some Caithness roe venison in the larder.

Over recent years the roe deer population in Caithness has increased dramatically. For a land containing little in the way of trees this is quite remarkable and somewhat out of character for the species. The roe have found the open, boggy moors and adjoining rough arable ground very suitable for their needs with the extensive reed beds providing cover that is ideal for their requirements. These moorland roe seem to have a greater tendency to feed during the day and may be seen wandering out in the open at all hours of the day.

Off the Scottish mainland there are many islands. Orkney in the north is a fascinating place to visit with its own unique character. It offers some moderate wildfowling and rough-shooting but has little to interest the shooter

wishing quality sport.

Much further south, out to the west of Argyll, lies the island of Islay, probably the most productive of all the islands for the sportsman. Islay has a wide variety of terrain from mountain and moorland to good quality arable. It has good red deer stalking, as do several of the islands, but it excels in the variety of its mixed shooting, and its woodcock and snipe are legendary. This island also acts as host to the largest British population of barnacle geese. This attractive black and white goose is a protected species, a fact which disgusts many Islay farmers who grudge the valuable grass which these birds consume.

The adjoining island of Jura is largely the province of a few wealthy landowners. Much of its area is devoted to deer forest, and it also carries a substantial stock of impressive wild goats.

The next island north of any significance is Mull. This is the premier island for the deer-stalker and there are many well-established estates where one of the principal economic activities is deerstalking. Mull formed the setting for the traditional epic tale of *The Muckle Hart of Benmore*, a beast of massive proportions that evaded its hunters for years and was finally brought down after a heroic pursuit on the slopes of Ben More. One of the pleasures of being on Mull is to see the abundance of predatory birds which exist there. At times there seems to be a buzzard on every telegraph pole and it is usually possible to view a golden eagle somewhere. When stalking on Mull if one visits an area where a beast has been gralloched the previous day, there is often a scene reminiscent of the Serengeti. A bevy of buzzards, just like a flock of vultures, squabble and contest the pile of entrails with often more than one eagle joining in the mêlée. It is fairly obvious that the lack of any need to conserve small game, of which there is virtually none on Mull, removes any desire by keepers to reduce illegally the numbers of these fine birds.

Further north lies the island of Rhum which is owned by the Nature Conservancy Council and for many years has been the centre for scientific study into red deer. Being a captive but entirely wild population within a relatively small area, the red deer population of Rhum has provided an ideal basis for detailed scientific study.

Within sight of Rhum lies the island of Skye. The island has many attractions but good gameshooting is not one of them. It has a sparse grouse population and some reasonable deerstalking, but the only quarry species which it produces in any quantity is the rabbit.

Out to the north west lie the enchanting Western Isles. South Uist is well worth a visit from the shooter, principally for its very varied wildfowling with excellent snipe and wood-cock. It is notable for hosting the sole truly wild colony of breeding greylag geese in the United Kingdom. Wildlife on South Uist benefits from the limestone-rich machair to the west of the island. This is a relatively flat area of sandy and fertile soil with a high limestone content producing luxuriant vegetation and bringing a richness of feeding to its marshes and freshwater lochs, benefiting both wildfowl and trout.

North Uist is more acidic and is composed mainly of heather moorland. It has little to offer in the way of shooting other than a few lonesome grouse, a modest population of red deer and limited wildfowl.

To the north the magnificent island of Harris supplies the ideal material for shooting clothing but little in the way of sporting quarry for the shotgun. By contrast, the rifle shot could wish for no finer place to stalk the truly wild red deer. Although the beasts do not produce notable heads, as Harris is far from being a fertile environment, the ground on which they are pursued is superb. Awe-inspiring seascapes and mountain grandeur provide a setting for the sport that would be difficult to equal anywhere else in the world.

Lewis, 'The Long Island', provides modest but varied and exciting sport for the gameshot. It is mainly acidic ground with much moor-land and heather but it does have quite fertile pockets along its coastline, particularly on the eastern shore. It carries a reasonable stock of grouse in some areas, sufficient for some modest days over pointers. On occasion its woodcock and snipe shooting can be superb as it is a haven for migrants. Garynahine estate on the west of the island even used to supply driven pheasant shooting which is no mean feat on an island virtually devoid of trees.

One of the many pleasant features of the Western Isles is that they create an impression of being in a totally different world and time. The sportsman looking for something different will appreciate a foray to the Islands. The islanders are a warm and hospitable people and make visitors extremely welcome. Gaelic is the official language used in local authority business and the everyday tongue of the local people, who have their own customs and way of life. Long may it remain so.

THE MARKET PLACE

It is not easy for the uninformed potential sporting visitor to Scotland to discover how to obtain access to the wide variety of game-shooting and deerstalking facilities which are available for lease. It is the purpose of this book to assist the visitor in finding suitable sport and to provide a background to the ways in which it is managed, with an insight into and an understanding of the long traditions and etiquette which surround it. To under-stand how the sport is operated on a commercial basis it is probably helpful to look at how this aspect of shooting has developed since gold first changed hands in exchange for sporting rights.

In the early 1800s, when gameshooting and deerstalking first came to be regarded as a form of recreation rather than just a means of obtaining wild meat, landowners and lairds found that their social life could be greatly extended and enlivened by inviting guests to share the sport on their land. The advent of the breech-loading gun and the development of large-scale game rearing extended the social possibilities. Instead of having a walk round and shooting a few head of game over dogs with three or four companions when the head of game on the ground was totally unpredict-able, reared pheasants and driven shooting presented many new opportunities.

The day of the grand country house party had dawned. That leader of fashion, the Prince of Wales, had developed a passion for the sport of driven shooting and this set the seal of approval on the sport which high society took to with gusto. The beauty of it was that ample sport could be guaranteed and hosts could plan a series of country house parties throughout the winter. They knew that protocol demanded that their guests issue return invitations and that by this system they would be ensured of a substantial round of social gatherings and a variety of sport throughout the winter. The pheasant, above all other creatures with the possible exception of the fox, has had a unique effect on British upper class social life. This bird indirectly caused a whole new pattern of social interaction among the landowning classes which still flourishes today.

As the sport of driven shooting developed, Scottish lairds rapidly became highly desirable social acquaintances. Many a Norfolk squire went to great pains to cultivate the friendship of his highland counterpart, provided of course that he owned a respectable grouse moor and had a decent staggie or two about his property. As is the way of Anglo-Saxons, the English squires did not take kindly to grovelling to their cousins north of the border for a bit of sport; they had to own it for themselves. Thus began the Scottish country property boom.

Like the Cheviot a century earlier, so the interests of stag and grouse soon dominated all other forms of highland land use. Unlike the effect that the clearances had, when ground turned over to sheep production drove many people from the land, the new Saxon landlords brought people back into the glens and established their own new serfdoms.

The establishment of the new sporting estates spawned a whole new underclass of servant. A multitude of new jobs was created and a novel career structure began to develop for rural working people which traditional agriculture and fishing had never provided. An entirely new industry sprang up which had considerable economic implications and brought much financial benefit to many rural areas.

A local lad could start life as a kennel boy and graduate to becoming head keeper of an estate and pony boys could work their way up to be head stalker. Lots of jobs were created. Where an estate had salmon fishing rights even more staff were needed and the sporting season was extended. Ponymen, dog-handlers, gillies, under-keepers, under-stalkers, head keepers, head stalkers and factors (a Scottish term for estate manager or agent) were all required on the sporting side. The great houses of the day required parlour-maids, chambermaids, kitchen-maids, cooks, housekeepers, butlers, and so on. The highland sporting estate became an institution in the land and despite its perpetuation of an almost feudal system it did, without doubt, help to reduce the population drift from country to town.

Originally the owners managed their sporting estates solely for the benefit of themselves, their families and guests. It soon became obvious to those with a bit of business acumen that they were not utilising this tremendous asset to the full and that they could readily lease some of the sporting to tenants which helped to offset the enormous cost of running their highland empires. Initially, it was normal for tenants to lease the total sportings on an estate including shootings, fishings, use of the estate house or sporting lodge and the full complement of staff. The usual letting period was for a complete month, sometimes even the whole season.

The sporting estates flourished until the onset of the First World War when all of the younger keepers and stalkers were called away to turn their rifles on a different kind of target. Things were never quite the same thereafter, and the huge estates were never again to employ the large retinues of staff that they had in the early 1900s.

The Second World War saw a great run-down in most of the large estates as yet again many of their staff went away to war and many did not come back. In the stringent times that followed there were not the resources to manage the estates in the good old style and many owners had difficulty keeping their lands intact. Gradually as times grew easier, sport began to take a higher priority. As in the days of Edward VII, when as Prince of Wales he encouraged a fashionable participation in shooting, so the Royal Family's custom of taking an annual holiday at Balmoral, where they took an active part in shooting and stalking, fuelled an upsurge of interest in the highland sporting holiday.

Increased leisure time and the growth of general affluence, coupled with a growing breakdown of social barriers, created an upswing of interest in fieldsports. Previously regarded as the prerogative of the upper classes, increasingly the pursuit of grouse and deer became socially and financially within reach of all levels of British society. Gradually it dawned on many hard-up landowners that letting the sport that they did not require themselves was a worthwhile financial undertaking. Demand from overseas began to grow in the 1960s and since then there has been an increasing demand to lease time on grouse moors and deer forests. On most estates, pheasant shooting took place on a serious basis on only a few days each season and therefore it was difficult for an estate to offer this form of sport on a commercial basis. As pheasant rearing methods became more efficient, so owners' thoughts turned to running commercial shooting days which could offset the cost of their own sport. The advent of demand for corporate entertainment and the growth of the sporting agencies helped to make driven pheasant shooting widely available on a commercial basis. The hotel and catering trade began to realise the commercial possibilities of being able to offer sporting facilities to their guests and as the demand for all forms of shooting grew so a service developed to meet this need.

The day of the sporting agent had dawned and, where previously landowners had been obliged to deal directly with sporting tenants or through their factors or land agents, now they could have all their sport professionally handled by an agency.

The commercialisation of shooting is now a well-established industry in Scotland creating considerable economic benefits for many rural areas. With the recent run-down in agricultural production and the development of 'set-aside' schemes, fieldsports have grown to be a very significant part of the agricultural and rural economy. A golden opportunity now exists for more sympathetic land use. The non-shooting public, even those opposed to field-sports, have in the past benefited indirectly by the status which gameshooting has been accorded by landowners. It is indisputable that

HIGH SUMMER. A fine stag in velvet. (*Perthshire Tourist Board*)

PINKFEET DROPPING
in to an
Aberdeenshire loch.
(*John Andrews*)

the shooting interest has ensured the maintenance of a quality landscape and the conservation of a diverse habitat for all forms of wildlife. In the past years of necessarily highly intensive agriculture, our non-commercial woodlands, hedgerows and wetlands would undoubtedly have suffered drastically and much more of this desirable habitat would have disappeared had it not been for the incentive of their value for game production. For example, most people would regard the 'bonnie purple heather' of the Scottish hills as an entirely natural asset. It is not generally realised that it is grouse shooting which was originally responsible for the development and maintenance of the vast expanse of healthy heather that blankets much of Scotland's uplands. The picture postcard manufacturers and songwriters have much to thank the grouse for. The common heather (*Calluna vulgaris*), although an indigenous plant, is basically a crop which, like any other, requires good husbandry to produce the optimum return. Heather husbandry is a very 'green' form of land use as it has no need of toxic chemicals to boost the crop and to discourage parasites. As well as being essential for high output grouse production, a moor with a patchwork of nutritious young growth and mixed ages of heather, well-drained and with a controlled population of predators is also an ideal habitat for numerous other species of wildlife and provides high quality grazing for a balanced number of sheep. Moors where efficient 'grouse farming' is practised generate the highest possible financial return for the landowner with substantial

economic benefits for the surrounding area. The wildlife and scenic value elements have an incalculable value to the general public that once lost can never be regained. The bleak alternative for much of the Scottish hill is total submersion beneath the alien conifer.

Considerable pressures exist from altruistic but sadly misguided people who would impose their will on the shooting public to prevent them from carrying out their traditional and legitimate sports. Visitors coming to Scotland to shoot should be reassured in the knowledge that they are contributing to the conservation of the Scottish landscape and its multifarious wildlife and that they are helping to maintain the viability of rural communities.

There is a variety of sources of and means by which the visitor may obtain good quality sport in Scotland. Some of the major estates, particularly where there is a knowledgeable factor, will organise the letting of all their own sport and the prospective client must deal directly with the estate. Some specialist hotels have long-established arrangements with local estates and landowners and will have a range of shooting and stalking that is available to their guests. There are now several well-established businesses in Scotland of full-time sporting agents that maintain a register of all types of sport and offer a fully professional service. Several of these agents will supply the visiting sportsman's every need including arranging the sport, accommodation, transport, equipment, clothing, ammunition, dealing with shot game and taxidermy, acting as sponsor to enable overseas visitors to obtain a temporary British gun or firearms certificate and some

will even arrange evening entertainment. The following chapters deal separately with all the varying game species and give details of specialist suppliers of the relevant sport.

In addition to those who are more directly involved, several of the major land agents in Scotland have now included a sporting agency as one of their services. These agencies act as an intermediary between sporting client and landowner. They are able to offer a comprehensive service and will have a register containing a wide range of shooting, stalking and fishing available for let. Many of the sporting leases which they have available will include a range of accommodation that may be an essential part of the package or may be optional. Accommodation varies greatly and may range from stately historic castles to humble 'but and bens'. Prospective tenants are able to register with these agencies and will receive regular circulars detailing the availability of sportings. Naturally, they also charge a commission.

The following companies offer this specialist type of service:

Finlayson Hughes

Contact: Simon Cadzow, Sporting Dept, Finlayson Hughes, 29 Barossa Place, Perth. Tel: 0738 25134/5.

Bell-Ingram

Contact: Peter Keyser or Patricia Grieve, Bell-Ingram, Durn, Isla Road, Perth, PH2 7HF. Tel: 0738 21121. Fax: 0738 30904.

2 The Law

GAME LICENCES

VISITORS TO SCOTLAND should note the following basic points of law that apply to gameshooting and deerstalking.

Any person wishing to shoot any game species in Scotland, including all species of deer, must hold a current game licence. These are available at any Crown Post Office and cost £6 for an annual licence (expiring 31 July), £4 for the period 1 August to 31 October, £4 for the period 1 November to 31 July, and £2 for a period of 14 days. These licences are solely a form of taxation and do not confer upon the holder any right whatsoever to enter any land for the purpose of pursuing game or any other species. In addition to a game licence, permission from the landowner or holder of the shooting rights is necessary before any person may legally enter land with a weapon in pursuit of game.

GAME SPECIES AND STATUTORY SHOOTING SEASONS

Pheasant:	1 October–1 February inclusive.
Partridge:	1 September– 1 February inclusive.
Grouse:	12 August–10 December inclusive.
Blackgame:	20 August–10 December inclusive.
Hare:	no close season but may not be offered for sale from 1 March–31 July inclusive.

It is illegal to shoot any species out of season, and to shoot game on Sundays, Christmas Day or at night. It is legal for hares and rabbits to be shot at night by authorised persons.

OTHER QUARRY SPECIES AND SEASONS

Capercaillie:	1 October–31 January inclusive.
Woodcock:	1 September–31 January inclusive.
Common snipe:	12 August–31 January inclusive.
Duck and geese (inland):	1 September–31 January inclusive.
Duck and geese (foreshore):	1 September–20 February.
Red deer stag:	1 July–20 October.
Red deer hind:	21 October–15 February.
Roe deer buck:	1 April–20 October.
Roe deer doe:	21 October–31 March.
Fallow deer buck:	1 August–30 April.
Fallow deer doe:	21 October–15 February.
Sika deer stag:	1 July–20 October.
Sika deer hind:	21 October–15 February.
Wild goat:	no close season.
Rabbit:	no close season.

Pigeon and the Crow Family

At the time of going to press there is no close season for woodpigeon, feral pigeon, collared dove, great and lesser blackbacked gull, herring gull and all members of the crow family - rook, carrion crow, hooded crow, magpie, jackdaw and jay, with the exception of the raven which is protected at all times. These species are currently on the pest list and may be shot at any time of year by persons having permission to shoot from the owner of the ground.

The Government has proposed changes to the Wildlife and Countryside Act 1981 which would involve scrapping the present pest list, introducing a close season for these species and setting up a licensing system which would permit these species to be killed only by holders of licences. This legislation is proposed solely because there is pressure on the British Government from the European beaurocrats in Brussels for the United Kingdom to fall in line with the 1979 European Community Birds Directive. None of the species concerned is in the slightest danger of having its population reduced to a critical level by sportsmen and game preservers, and there is no practical conservation reason for this unnecessary and cumbersome piece of EC legislative nonsense.

The national shooting and conservation organisations – the Game Conservancy Council, the British Association for Shooting and Conservation, and the British Field Sports Society are strongly objecting to these proposals which the Government wishes to introduce by 1 December 1990. At the present time it is not known what the outcome will be.

In Scotland it is illegal to shoot any of the above mentioned species on Sundays or on Christmas Day.

CUSTOMARY SHOOTING PERIODS

Visitors to Scotland, particularly those from North America, may well be surprised at the length of the gameshooting seasons. The fact that the statutory open season for most game species extends for a full four months of the autumn and winter allows for a well-spaced programme of shooting days to be arranged throughout the season by most shoot managers. Therefore this situation is very well suited to the sporting visitor who may select the timing of a shooting holiday from a wide range of dates. Although the seasons are extensive it should be understood that organised shooting does not necessarily take place throughout the whole of the official open season. In several cases serious shooting does not start until well into the season and may

cease several weeks prior to the close. It may be helpful to be aware of the general trends in the shooting calendar.

Grouse

Practically everybody knows that the grouse season starts on 12 August and in normal practice shooting starts on this date. It should be noted that many estates do not commence driven shooting until nearer to the end of August and the opening days may be solely confined to walked up shooting up over dogs. This is a reasonable way of dealing with the stock of birds, as in a season starting with a late cold spring the coveys may not be fully developed by the twelfth and it makes sense to delay the serious cull of the stock of birds on the moor until later when they will be stronger on the wing and provide better sport. In any event, shooting grouse over pointers is a form of sport which is growing in popularity. This may be due in part to its considerably lower cost than driven shooting, but is probably very much influenced by nostalgia for the traditions of yesteryear and the growing interest in all forms of dog work. By late September the grouse do not hold so well for the dogs and are inclined to become much wilder. By October they are generally too wild to be approached within range by walking up and then the only way to reduce the stock to a suitable breeding density is by driving. Traditionally the majority of driven grouse shooting in Scotland takes place from late August to mid-October, and although the season extends to 10 December, in practice few grouse drives take

place after mid-October. Standing frozen stiff in a butt at 2,000 ft in a north-easterly gale is not everyone's idea of fun, but these conditions would present birds of a quality that would test any sportsman to the utmost. On the few estates where grouse drives are organised in November the shooting thus presented is probably the most exciting and challenging shotgun sport to be had in the United Kingdom and truly separates 'the men from the boys'.

In considering the statutory grouse season, it is difficult to refrain from wondering whether the decision to start early in the year and to close early was influenced more by thoughts for the comfort and convenience of Victorian sportsmen than for the welfare of their quarry.

Pheasant

The pheasant is a big bird and requires some time to attain physical maturity. Even by the start of the season on 1 October there are few birds of the year that are anything more than large poults. Leaving them for a couple more weeks makes a dramatic difference to their size and eating quality. Those who excuse the shooting of young pheasants in the opening days of the season by claiming that they are sweet and excellent eating are being deliberately misleading in an attempt to hide their greed and selfish behaviour. There is no gastronomic delight in a pitiful creature with a breast like a razor blade and flesh like boiled string. Pheasants need to have several weeks of stuffing themselves on the barley and wheat stubbles and benefiting from the wild fruits of oak and beech before they are worthy of the chef. They are at their best in November and December when they have had a taste of the good life, put on maximum weight and are carrying a surplus of rich yellow fat. Then they are food for the gods. If pheasant shooting must take place in the opening days of October it is acceptable if confined to old cock birds. They may be recognised by their well-developed plumage and in particular by the length of their tails. With hen birds it is not so easy to differentiate instantly between mature females and birds of the year, and they are best left until later in the season.

The general trend with driven pheasant shooting is for it not to commence in any serious way until late October at the earliest. Many estates do not start until well into November which has the advantage of better visibility for the shooter as the leaf is off most species of tree by then, and as the birds are more mature they will fly faster and higher and be superior on the table to those killed in October. To the seasoned pheasant shooter there is nothing to beat the challenge of driven birds in January, particularly if there is a good hard wind blowing. There is a vast difference between sport such as this and blasting some unfortunate poult up the backside as it blunders out almost underfoot from an October turnip field.

In the latter half of January it is a traditonal management practice on many estates to restrict the shooting to cock birds only in order to conserve as many hens as possible to breed in the following spring. Such shooting is known as 'cocks only' days and on many shoots a traditional penalty is imposed on any unhappy shooter who accidently kills a hen bird. This penalty is paid to the keeper who sometimes does quite well as up to £20 per bird may be charged. With driven shooting in particular it is sometimes none to easy to differentiate between cocks and hens as the birds are often seen mainly in silhouette by the shooter without the benefit of viewing the different colouration of the sexes. In particular it is very easy to mistake a dark melanistic hen for a cock bird and on 'cocks only' days many a keeper has made a tidy sum by having plenty of this grouse-coloured type of hen pheasant on his ground. On these occasions some of the more wickedly inclined beaters will enter into the spirit of the thing by saluting each hen bird that heads over the guns with cries of 'Cock over!'.

Partridge

In the good old days before our farmlands became chemically treated, sanitised deserts, 1 September was a notable date: it signalled the start of the partridge season. Time was when each of the typical small fields of the time, surrounded as they were by thick sheltering hedges, held one or two good-sized coveys of native grey partridge. The dawn of 1 September saw top-hatted and frock-coated sporting gentlemen slung about with shot and powder flask setting afield with their trusty percussion weapons and several brace of eager setters to garner some of the season's bountiful harvest of wild partridge.

Came the day of demand for high agricultural output, and the land was forced to be subject to all the horrors of intensive productivity. This did not suit the partridge. Gone were the myriad insects on which the chicks were so dependent in their crucial early days and gone was much of the friendly shelter and safe nesting of the many rough corners and hedgerows. Partridge stocks declined dramatically and from its position as the premier low-ground gamebird the partridge featured but spasmodically in the shooting calendar in all but a few favoured and well-managed areas. The French or redleg partridge began to usurp the native grey in many areas, principally because it is so much easier to rear in quantity. In recent years, due to much improve management, driven partridge shooting again features prominently in the sporting programme of many low-ground estates, although in Scotland the bird has never had quite the position that it holds across the border in England.

In practice, serious driven partridge does not start until towards the end of September as even in good summers the young birds are seldom of a size to warrant shooting on the opening day. Driven shooting of the wild grey partridge is normally carried out from late September until around the end of November. Shooting of redlegs may take place throughout the whole partridge season because unlike the native greys there is not the same incentive to leave a breeding stock on the ground, since these 'foreigners' are inclined to wander far and wide from their original release points.

Wildfowl

In the same bygone era that top-hatted sportsmen sallied forth to the stubble fields on 1 September, the wildfowling enthusiast of the day had already enjoyed a full month of legal slaughter. The duck season used to open on the infamous 1 August when the ritual execution of 'flappers' would take place. The majority of home-bred duck of the year would be quite immature by the start of August and even most of the adults would still be recovering from the annual moult which removed their ability to fly. Neither young nor old could take to the air and were easy prey for the rapacious gunner of the day.

Fortunately, current legislation has now delayed the opening of the wildfowl season until 1 September, but even at this time there are many immature birds around and considerable restraint should be exercised in the early days of the season.

Migrant duck do not begin to appear in Scotland until towards the end of September. The big flocks of widgeon from Iceland, Scandinavia and northern USSR begin to arrive at that time and numbers increase in response to severe weather conditions in these areas and as the autumn and winter progress. The peak number of migrant duck is reached around late December which is quite convenient for the wildfowler, as these welcome visitors top up the numbers of native born duck and add to the possibilities of sport, producing extra variety. Duckshooting and in particular coastal wildfowling, because it is not solely dependent on a resident population,

carries on unabated throughout the season up until the close of inland shooting on 31 January. Those hardy souls who pursue their sport around the coast below the high water mark have an extra three weeks in which to shoot ducks and geese before the complete closure of wildfowling on 20 February. This coastal extension of the season applies only to geese and duck and not to other species of wildfowl such as waders. It should be noted that it is illegal to shoot from a mechanically propelled boat in the immediate pursuit of wildfowl. There is no shooting of wildfowl in Scotland on Sundays or on Christmas Day.

Because wildfowl are more vulnerable to prolonged periods of hard weather when severe frosts may dramatically restrict their access to many food sources, it should be noted that under the provisions of the Wildlife and Countryside Act 1981 periods of special protection may be introduced. At any time during the open season when there are extended periods of exceptionally hard frost there could be a total national ban on shooting all species of wildfowl. The most likely time for such a ban to be imposed is during January or February and there have been several occasions in recent years when this additional form of protection has been necessary. Such orders are made by the Secretary of State in consultation with the national sporting and conservation organisations and are made known throughout the media.

Basically gooseshooting takes place whenever the opportunity arises. Being somewhat ephemeral creatures with a 'here today and gone tomorrow' lifestyle it is difficult to

predict exactly when geese will be present in a particular area. This fact should be borne in mind when arranging a specific gooseshooting trip. Although the season opens on 1 September, very rarely is it that migrant birds will have arrived in Scotland by that time. The arrival of the first pinkfeet is invariably very predictable as the first skeins are to be seen in Scotland around 15 and 16 September. Numbers rapidly build up to a peak around mid-October which is when the first main concentrations of greylag begin to put in an appearance. The numbers of migrant greys build up to a peak in Scotland around mid-November. So October and November are the most reliable months for coming to grips with pinkfeet, and November and December are likely to be the most productive months for sport with greylags.

Red Deer

Much of the legislation governing the sport of deerstalking in Scotland is laid down by the Deer (Scotland) Act 1959 and the subsequent Deer (Amendment) (Scotland) Act 1982. These statutes lay down specific and separate close seasons for both stags and hinds. The period when red deer stags may be killed in Scotland is from 1 July to 20 October inclusive while the open season for hinds is from 21 October to 15 February inclusive.

Although the stag season opens in July, in practice red deer stag stalking does not really start in earnest on most estates until August. Most stags will still be in velvet in July and will not reach their maximum body weight until near the end of the summer. Until the commencement of the rut towards the end of September, stags will normally be found in 'men only' groups often occupying the highest ground available to them. Their predeliction for the remote and less accessible places makes their pursuit more arduous and time-consuming early in the season. The highest demand for stag stalking is inclined to be from late September until the end of the season. This is the most exciting time to be on the hill as the rutting season is in full swing, there is a constant movement of stags and on most estates they will be on the lower ground and more accessible to the stalker. If difficulty is experienced in obtaining stag stalking in September and October the month of August should not be disregarded as there are many factors in favour of this time. There is rather less demand for sport at that time and if the visiting stalker is reasonably fit the extra challenge of seeking a stag on the high ground may be very worthwhile. In August the days are longer and usually the weather is more congenial than it is in later Autumn. To stalk a stag on the 'high tops' on a clear August day when the view stretches for miles around is a superb sporting experience.

Hind stalking normally gets underway rapidly as soon as the season is open. Most estates will wish to secure their annual cull of hinds before the hard weather sets in and makes the approach to the beasts and subsequent outward transport of the carcasses so much more difficult. Early in the season the hinds are in peak condition which is a factor to be considered when the sale of venison is of

economic importance to an estate. Hind stalking is at its peak in November and December and is most likely to be available to the visiting stalker at these times. The worst weather on the Scottish hill is generally experienced after Christmas so these factors should be taken into account when planning a hind stalking trip.

Whereas the bulk of stag stalking is normally let by the week with tenants often retaining the same week year after year, hind stalking is often more readily available and it makes a good introduction to the sport of red deer stalking for the newcomer. It is easier to arrange single day stalking for hinds than for stags and it is not so costly.

Roe Deer

The season in which it is legal to shoot roe-buck is from 1 April to 20 October inclusive. In former years tradition and custom had it that most stalking of roebuck did not take place until May as many buck were not clear of velvet until then. As older bucks are some-times 'clean' in April there are some places where stalking does take place in the first legal month. The preferred period for stalking roe-buck is from May until early August. In the earlier months not only is it light very early in the morning, the prime time of day for stalking, but the vegetation has not grown to its fullest extent enabling the deer to be much more easily spied than later on in the year. The dreaded Scottish midges are not so active earlier in the year and in the late summer their depredations on the stalker's blood supply can

turn a pleasant early morning or late evening stalk into a nightmare. From midsummer onwards other winged creatures can inflict misery on the roe stalker, as anyone who has ever gralloched a deer in woodland at that time will tell you. Dense clouds of bluebottles buzzing round the head and up the nose, as with bloodied hands the stalker vainly tries to drive them hence, is not a pleasurable experience. Where there are roe on open moorland and no problem with obscuring vegetation, stalking may be continued until the close of the season in October. Techniques are similar to red deer stalking and often these roe of the wide expanses continue to be active throughout the day, making daytime stalking a reasonable proposition.

Open season for roe does is from 21 October to 31 March inclusive. On most estates there is no preferred time to carry out the female cull but it is easier to see the deer in woodland once the frost has knocked down the vegetation and the leaf is off the trees, which is normally the case after mid-November. It should be possible to arrange to stalk roe does at any time within the legal season.

Wild Goats, Sika and Fallow Deer

There is no statutory close season for wild goats and they may legally be shot at any time. In practice it is normally only the billy goat which is of interest to the sportsman, usually during the month of June and from August to November. It is rarely that the female nanny goat is shot for sporting purposes, but if this does take place then the usual period is

M UIRBURN.
HEATHER
management by burning
off old plants to promote
nourishing new growth.
(*Neil McIntyre*)

R ED GROUSE cock.
(*Sport in Scotland*)

October/November when the young kids of the year are able to fend for themselves.

Sika stags have the same statutory season as red deer stags so a stalking programme may be arranged where it is possible to shoot both species and this even extended to include fallow buck. Sport in Scotland Ltd offer a number of mixed bag programmes such as this (see chapter 15). Normally sika stag stalking is offered from September to the end of the season on 20 October and sika hinds from 21 October until Christmas time.

Fallow buck have a long statutory season which recognises the fact that the males do not lose condition after the rut in October to the same extent that red stags do. The usual period for stalking fallow bucks is mid-October to the end of November. Fallow does are normally shot from the start of their open season on 21 October to around the end of December.

PROHIBITED METHODS OF TAKING QUARRY SPECIES

It is prohibited to take quarry species by using any of the following:
1 Any automatic or semi-automatic weapon.
2 Any shotgun of which the barrel has an internal diameter at the muzzle of more than 1¾ in (4.5 cm).
3 Any device for illuminating a target.
4 Any form of artificial lighting or any mirror or other dazzling device.
5 A decoy by means of any sound recording, or any live bird, or animal which is tethered, or which is secured by means of braces or other similar appliances, or which is blind, maimed or injured.
6 Any mechanically propelled vehicle in immediate pursuit of a wild bird for the purpose of killing or taking that bird.

UK FIREARMS AND SHOTGUN LEGISLATION

Shotguns

A shotgun certificate is required by anyone who wishes to possess, acquire or use a shotgun. Application forms and full details of requirements are obtainable from local police stations, but the applicant must be of good character, a fact which must be endorsed by a responsible person. A shotgun certificate covers all smooth-bore weapons with barrels longer than 24 in (60 cm) and pump-action and semi-automatic weapons which have a magazine capacity not exceeding two shots. Production of a shotgun certificate is necessary to purchase weapons and ammunition.

Rifles

Anyone wishing to possess, acquire or use a rifle must obtain a firearms certificate from their local chief officer of police. Application forms are obtainable from local police stations. It is necessary to indicate what calibre and type of weapon the applicant intends to acquire and applicants must show that they have legitimate reason for requiring the weapon. The main essential when applying for a firearms certificate is to be able to produce confirmation that the applicant has permission from the owner of the ground on which he intends to use the weapon. The ground in question must be suitable for the purpose specified. The application must be endorsed by some pillar of society who knows the applicant personally, such as a police officer, minister, doctor or Justice of the Peace. Recent photographs of the applicant must also be supplied. The applicant must have no criminal record.

The law regarding the importation and use of firearms and shotguns by foreign nationals changed on 31 September 1989. In order to get a permit for one year for a rifle or shotgun a foreign national must have a UK sponsor who must apply for the permit(s). This can be arranged through companies such as Sport in Scotland Ltd who can act as sponsor for their clients. They will send a form which must be completed and returned along with £20 per shotgun permit and £20 per rifle permit. More than one weapon can be included in each type of permit. Enough time must be allowed for documents to be processed and returned by post. It is recommended that shooting visitors to Scotland who wish to bring their own weapons with them should give at least two months notice to their UK sponsor in order to allow adequate time for the necessary permits to be processed.

3 Arms, Ammunition and Equipment for the Shotgunner

WEAPONS FOR THE GAMESHOOTER

THE TRADITIONAL ARM for gameshooting in the UK is the side-by-side, double-barrelled hammerless ejector gun. This is made in two main actions – the boxlock and the sidelock. Most boxlocks are generally built on the robust and trouble-free, if slightly clumsy and weighty, Anson and Deeley action. Because this action is relatively simple to produce boxlocks are normally modestly priced guns and are regarded as the everyday workhorse gun, whereas sidelocks are generally very expensive in keeping with their position as the pinnacle of the gunmaker's craft. The British sidelock is much more than just a weapon for discharging shot; it is very much a work of art, a fact which is recognised by their investment value. There are many world-famous makers of these 'best' guns, as they are known in the trade, and this marriage of intricately engraved steel and finest root walnut into a practical working tool that will virtually never wear out is British craftsmanship at its incomparable best. When handling one of these delightful creations it is difficult to appreciate that this functional artistry has been brought to this state of perfection purely by the lengthy process of hand filing and fitting of steel together with the chiselling and shaping of a raw block of wood by two or three craftsmen, employing almost exclusively small hand tools. There is virtually no machining involved, other than in the initial preparation of the basic steel tubes, and the primary formation of the action block. Other than the lighter weight and superior handling qualities of 'best' guns, there is no practical difference between boxlocks and sidelocks in their performance in the field or in their suitability for gameshooting.

Most of the British shotguns in use today were made at least 50 years ago and many of those still in constant action will be closer to 100 years old. This says a great deal for the quality of the craftsmanship and materials used in their production and also endorses the durability of the designs to which these guns were built. The last quarter of the nineteenth century was a particularly prolific period for British gunmaking and many of the inventions patented at that time are still used in exactly their original form. Throughout the world most sporting gun production today incorporates British designs from this period, designs which have stood the test of time and have remained unchanged for the last century.

Virtually all the guns used today in organised Scottish shooting will be of the modern hammerless variety, a design which was first introduced around 1860, but occasionally some eccentric may turn up with an old hammer gun. These were the common sporting arm up until the late 1800s and due to the superb quality of the British-made gun many good conditioned examples survive to this day. They are perfectly safe if used by a shooter who is practised in handling them but devotees of hammer guns are inclined to be given a wide berth due to the weapon's rather undeserved reputation for accidental discharges. Safety is very much a paramount consideration in the UK shooting field and anything which may be regarded as presenting a hazard to life and limb is most unwelcome.

Over and unders are perfectly acceptable on the formal shooting scene in Scotland, although the less expensive versions from Russia and Europe are inclined to be looked down on somewhat. British makers did produce a few 'best' guns in over and under action which started to gain in popularity in

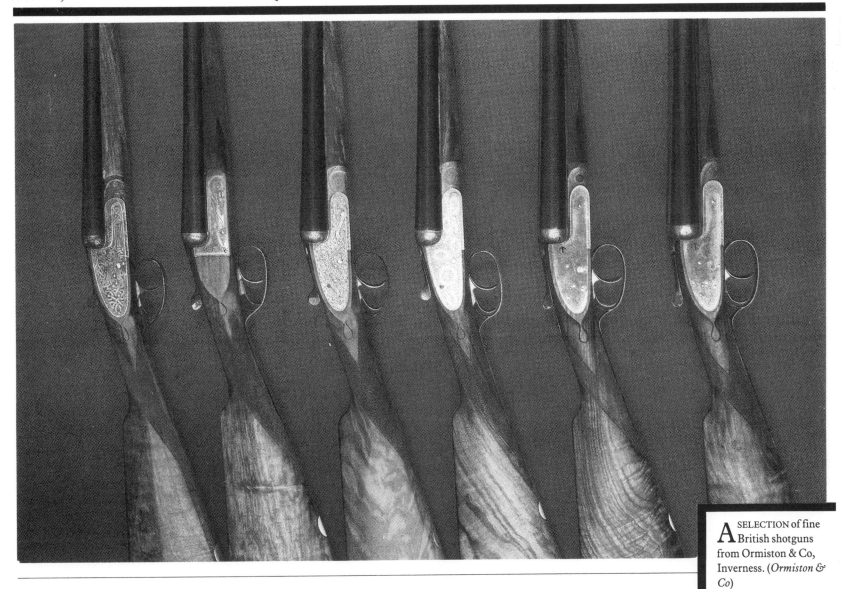

A SELECTION of fine British shotguns from Ormiston & Co, Inverness. (*Ormiston & Co*)

the early 1900s, and, perhaps because relatively few examples were made, they are much sought after today. Some British makers will still take commissions to produce these super-imposed barrel guns if the client has the necessary wherewithal. Virtually all non-British over and unders are chambered for the 2¾in load and are inclined to be heavier than most side-by-sides. One major disadvantage in formal shooting of an over and under is that it is not quite so easy to reload quickly due to the extra travel that the barrels must make before bringing the ejectors into use. This may prove to be irritating during hectic action and in the confined space of a grouse butt. In addition, on a sweaty August day whilst walking the heather hill the shooter may regret the tendency of many over and unders to be a little on the heavy side.

The most popular bore or gauge for all types of gameshooting in Scotland is the 12. The vast majority of British guns were made in this bore, designed to be used in conjunction with the 2½in load but the smaller 16, 20 or 28 bores may be used with only a minor loss of efficiency. The handy little 20 bore is becoming increasingly popular due to its light weight and minimal recoil, which is of benefit without a great deal of loss in practical range or efficiency, even using standard 2½in loads. The 20 is an ideal bore for ladies, the elderly or young entrants to the sport. Similar comments may be made of the 16 and 28 bores, but like for like the 16 is only a shade lighter than the 12 and cartridges for it are sometimes not so readily available. The 28 bore is a delightful little weapon but it takes a

very skilled and experienced shot to perform really well with it and its cartridges are not easy to obtain in some areas.

Any type of repeating shotgun or so-called 'automatic' would be a very bad choice for the majority of shooting situations in Scotland. The only merit that these guns possess, apart from their relatively low cost, is their higher than normal rate of fire-power which, in certain pigeon or wildfowling situations, could offer some advantage over the conventional two shot arm. In driven gameshooting the skilled operator of an ejecting double gun will discharge four shots for every five fired by an automatic. To appear with a self-loading gun on a formal Scottish shoot is certain to produce no kind of welcome at all. The main objection to automatics by traditionally minded 'Brits' (in addition to their undesirable origin in some foreign factory) is that it cannot clearly be demonstrated to neighbouring guns that the weapon is unloaded. It is also difficult for the user to check for obstructions in the barrel. The auto's potentially rapid rate of fire is considered by many to be 'not quite cricket'. Recent legislation virtually eliminated the semi-automatic shotgun in Britain as all self-loading smooth-bore weapons are now restricted by law to a capacity of two shots. Self-loading weapons that were previously capable of holding and firing up to five shots were required to have their magazines plugged and be restricted to two shot capability. The pump-action, that favourite weapon of the American upland gameshooter, is regarded in law as being in the same category as a semi-automatic and is equally looked on with

disfavour on most British formal shooting occasions. The American cops and robbers movie featuring the use of pump-actions as 'alley-cleaners' has not helped the image of the design as a sporting arm in this country. However, pump-actions do attract a little sympathy and regard from British shooters who really know their guns and are able to appreciate the quality of a good old Winchester '87.

If the shooter finds that he really must have a self-loading five shot gun, it is still theoretically possible for him to achieve this. Such weapons are now regarded in law in the same category as rifled firearms and it is necessary to go through the same lengthy and complicated process of applying for a firearms certificate in order to possess one. These days chief constables require a great deal of convincing that *any* applicant has a legitimate need for such a weapon.

For those in the big league who wish for an increased rate of fire the problem is easily solved, if expense is no object, by the use of a pair of perfectly matched conventional double guns and a nimble loader. A double gun shoot normally means that at times during the drives there will be so many birds coming over the guns a shooter armed with only one gun would miss many opportunities whilst reloading. Double guns are frequently employed on many of the high production grouse moors where the use of a matched pair of guns and a loader are often justified. On this type of moor the birds frequently come to the butts in sizeable coveys and the process of arranging and carrying out the drives is lengthy and complicated. There-

THE LAST drive of the day. (*John Andrews*)

A COMPETENT team for the grouse moor. English and Irish setters and handlers. (*Roger Tidman*)

G ROUSE WINDED. An English Pointer on point. (*Roger Tidman*)

O LD HEATHER provides good cover. (*Roger Tidman*)

COCK GROUSE crowing. (*Roger Tidman*)

THE START of grouse country. The Sma' Glen in Perthshire. (*Perthshire Tourist Board*)

TALLYING UP. The day's bag is transferred to the larder. (*John Andrews*)

BLACKCOCK AGGRO. Two cocks square up on the traditional 'lekking' ground. (*Neil McIntyre*)

fore the best use must be made of the shooting opportunities. Where there are really good grouse stocks the numbers must be reduced as a good management practice in order to keep the residual breeding stock at a healthy level. Shooting is the sole means of economically controlling grouse numbers and therefore it makes a deal of sense to specify the use of double guns where there is a need to shoot the maximum bag. To watch an experienced team of gun and loader dealing with a large covey of driven grouse by taking a left and right in front and expertly changing guns as they turn to take another two birds right and left behind the butt is to see gameshooting skill at its finest.

Double gun shooting is not quite so justifiable on pheasant shoots as it may occasionally encourage greed and the shooting of low or otherwise unsporting birds. There are few Scottish partridge shoots where the use of double guns is ever necessary although there are places in England where this does occur. Although most double gun shooting in Scotland involves the use of traditional British side-by-side guns there is no reason why pairs of well-matched over and unders should not be used, although this type of action does have the minor disadvantages already mentioned. The essential factor in double gun shooting is for both shooter and loader to work as a smoothly co-ordinated team and this does require some practice. There are occasional fiascos to be seen where neither gun nor loader really knows what he is doing and in a flurry of birds on a good grouse drive their desperate antics may well provide better sport for their neighbours than the shooting.

It is good to know that the ancient and honourable art of gunmaking is still alive and well in Scotland. In the late nineteenth century and up until the outbreak of the First World War several small gunmaking businesses could be found in every major Scottish town. Today there are but a handful of these superb craftsmen in steel and wood, but those who are fortunate to have been taught the trade from the fast disappearing breed of gunmaking craftsmen of yesteryear are far from struggling to ply their trade in a dingy garret. The few who have earned the time-honoured skills and knowledge gained from a long apprenticeship to be able to produce top quality guns to the traditionally high Scottish standard are in steady demand. Full order books are the norm and most clients will be fortunate if their commissions for new weapons are filled in less than two years.

Probably the best of all Scottish guns and arguably one of the finest in the world is the renowned Dickson Round Action. Made by the long-established Edinburgh gunmakers John Dickson & Sons, this is a most elegant, well-balanced and aesthetically pleasing gun. Of 'best' quality, it has a unique type of action, being neither sidelock nor boxlock. Unusually the locks on a Round Action are mounted on the trigger plate and contained within the head of the stock. An attractive feature of this novel design is that it permits the ejector mechanism to be located towards the rear of the gun, rather than being contained in the fore-end as in the majority of sidelocks. This brings more of the weight back into the hand, providing an additional benefit to the gun's superb handling qualities.

The business of John Dickson & Sons continues to flourish in Frederick Street in Edinburgh as suppliers of quality guns, rifles and fishing tackle. Sadly these days, the company's workshops are solely devoted to repairs, adjustments and renovations and are no longer the birthplace of the exquisite and uniquely Scottish shotgun. Fortunately all the skills of the Dickson gunmakers have not vanished to some Edinburgh graveyard. Round action guns to the Dickson design and quality continue to be built in Scotland today. David MacKay Brown is a gunmaker who served his apprenticeship with the famous Glasgow firm of Alexander Martin and subsequently finished his long indenture with John Dickson when the two companies amalgamated. He left to set up an independent workshop, and at Bothwell in Lanarkshire David produces the very fine MacKay Brown round action gun. Its equal in quality and made by the same painstaking process as the long-established Dickson, the MacKay Brown version is making a name worldwide for itself and its maker. So well-regarded is his work that David was commissioned by the Royal Armouries to build a round action for their collection. This gun is quite unique as it is engraved with illustrations of the legendary ravens of the Tower of London and has a most unusual overall decoration of engraved ravens' feathers. Secured for posterity in the Royal Armouries' collection in the Tower of London, this gun is the first modern masterpiece to join many fine examples of the ancient art of the armourer on display to the public for eternity. Today the price of skilled craftsmanship does not come cheaply but despite this many clients are prepared to wait the two years delivery time, determined to invest in these fine sporting weapons. David has a very healthy order book notwithstanding the £28,000 price tag. Far-sightedly, he is wisely training apprentices to follow in his footsteps. Thus the future of round action production in Scotland looks promising.

Daniel Fraser was another innovative Edinburgh maker of quality guns and rifles and happily, to the benefit of Scottish gun-making, his original designs also continue in production today. Fraser was born in Inverness in 1845 and moved to Edinburgh in 1858. In 1859, at the age of 13, he became apprenticed to the well-established and famous Edinburgh gunmaker Alexander Henry of St Andrew's Street who was a prolific producer of quality sporting weapons, many of which are still in constant use today. Fraser became an essential and highly skilled part of the Alex Henry firm until 1878 when, like so many of the highly talented craftsmen of the time, he left to set up a gunmaking business in his own right, the Dan'l Fraser Gun and Rifle Making Company at 18 Leith Walk, Edinburgh. Daniel Fraser was the recipient of a number of patents relating to the design and improvement of guns and rifles of the period. He was an exceptionally good rifle shot and was for most of his adult life a member of the Queen's Edinburgh Rifle Volunteer Brigade, representing Scotland on many occasions in competition. He enjoyed unparalleled acclaim

for the outstanding excellence of his own designs of guns and rifles, rapidly gaining a unique reputation as a riflemaker, specialising in sporting rifles which were the larger part of his production. In 1879 he obtained a patent for a particular type of hammerless shotgun which circumstances at the time indicate may well have influenced the subsequent design of the Dickson Round Action. He died in 1902 at the age of 57, the business being continued by his sons at the Edinburgh Leith address.

Today the Dan'l Fraser Company has returned to its founder's home area where guns and especially rifles continue to be built to the same enviable standard of quality that Daniel Fraser demanded. The company is based in the Black Isle near Inverness at Peddieston which lies between Rosemarkie and Cromarty, and currently it builds best quality shotguns with a delightfully Scottish style of Celtic engraving. Dan'l Fraser is recognised world-wide as a specialist in rifle design and manufacture, producing a unique new and improved design of falling block rifle action as well as the prestigious double-barrel rifles for which the company is renowned. The company works from what is probably one of the finest equipped gunmaking workshops in the country. It is run by Bernard Horton-Corcoran who, like Daniel Fraser before him, has received a number of awards and patents for his work in the design and manufacture of sporting arms. Visitors are welcome to view the company's workshops and a superb shooting school and clay shooting ground complete a most attractive facility for the sportsman.

BARREL LENGTH AND CHOKE

Everyone has personal views regarding the most suitable length of barrels and how they should be choked for the particular type of shooting engaged in. Barrel lengths in common use are 30in, 28in, 27in and 25in. Controversy about this has raged for years but undoubtedly for all-round shooting purposes the 28in barrelled gun would be a wise choice. In the days of black powder a long barrelled gun was inclined to give a marginally better performance than short barrels but when nitro powder came into common usage there was no practical ballistic difference. Robert Churchill, the famous London gunmaker, built and popularised the 'Churchill twenty-five', a short barrel lightweight gun with a very narrow file-cut rib. This was a very fast handling weapon, well suited to the physique of a short and stocky man like Robert Churchill. Great store is set by most gunmakers in having the stocks of their guns tailor-made to suit the physique, eyesight and shooting style of clients. A well-fitted gun is an undoubted advantage to efficient shooting and it would seem a logical extension of this premise that the barrel length should also match the physique of the shooter. There is also a case to be made for longer barrels for shooting high birds as such barrel length is inclined to encourage a smooth, steady and prolonged swing. Short barrels, in addition to producing a lighter gun, may assist on any occasion where swift 'snap-shooting' is required and the 'twenty-five' is often popular on the moor and in the grouse butt.

The choke of a shotgun is the degree by

which the barrels are constricted at the muzzle. After leaving the chamber at the breech end the bore is of uniform diameter until, at a few inches from the muzzle, the bore starts to narrow into a choke cone. There are varying degrees of constriction used and the tighter the choke becomes the more the shot is held together in its length of travel and the more pellets it will deliver into a 30in (76cm) circle at 40yd (37m). This is a standard measure of assessing the 'pattern' thrown by the barrels and a given degree of choke in a shotgun. The degrees of choke are full choke (the tightest constriction), three-quarter choke, half choke, quarter choke, one-eighth choke or improved cylinder, and true cylinder (no constriction at the muzzle, same internal bore diameter from chamber to muzzle).

In simplified terms, full choke is suited to maximum range shooting and a more open boring is designed for normal closer range work. A fully choked gun requires a greater degree of accuracy in use and another of the drawbacks of this tight boring is that if it is used on game at close or average range there will be so many pellets hitting the target that game will be smashed to pieces and be quite inedible. A good choice of choke boring for all round Scottish gameshooting would be for the gun to have improved cylinder in the right barrel and half choke in the left.

The majority of double-barrel guns are fitted with double triggers. The front trigger fires the right barrel first which is normally the more open boring and the back trigger fires the left, usually the barrel with the greater degree of choke. Over and unders are normally more open bored on the lower first firing barrel. Some driven grouse specialists prefer guns with the barrel having the tighter degree of choke to be the right or lower barrel, the first fired. Driven grouse are best taken in front and the first shot will be at the greater range. It is possible to find double-barrelled guns with single triggers and usually these are not selective. Over and unders offer a wider choice of trigger arrangements and many have single selective triggers. In practical terms such trigger mechanisms offer little advantage for gameshooting as there are few people who are capable of efficiently using the system to full potential and for normal shooters a single selective trigger can cause delays in smooth and efficient gun mounting and firing.

CARTRIDGES AND LOADS FOR GAMESHOOTING

Many and various are the cartridges and loads on offer to the gameshooter. In recent years there has been a great deal of competition for the UK cartridge market which was previously dominated by the British-made Eley-Kynoch range. The rapid increase in popularity of clay shooting in the UK has led to an enormous range of imported cartridges appearing on the market and fierce competition happily keeps prices at a reasonable level.

An essential safety factor to be borne in mind when matching load to gun is that the vast majority of British-made guns, particularly those of pre-1940 vintage, are chambered solely for the 2½ in (65 mm) load whereas many imported cartridges are 2¾ in (70 mm) loads. Most non-British-made guns are chambered for the 2¾ in (70 mm) load and 2½ in (65 mm) loads may be used in these with no problem. Although British or other makes of 2½ in chambered guns will accept and fire 2¾ in loads, these guns are not designed to cope with the higher pressures generated and thus such practice is extremely dangerous, running the risk of exploding barrels with obviously undesirable results for the careless shooter. The chamber size and loads for which a gun has been made and tested are usually indicated by the proof marks, which on a double gun are normally found on the barrel flats. Additional proof markings are normally impressed on the action. Unless a gun is specifically and clearly marked as being suitable for 2¾ or the heavier 3 in load, the safest practice is to use only 2½ in load cartridges. This should not be regarded in any way as a handicap. In any event such cartridges will be more than adequate for most shooting situations to be found in Scotland, with the possible exception of geese.

All British-made guns are required by law to undergo testing by one of the proof houses in London or Birmingham before being offered for sale. Similarly all foreign-made weapons are required to be subject to British proof, with the exception of American makes as the American proof is accepted by the British Proof House. It is a serious offence to offer for sale an unproved weapon and care has to be taken in this regard as a previously 'in proof' weapon may be rendered 'out of proof' by ill-treatment, damage or alteration. Because the introduction of new proof regulations and proof markings does not render earlier proof marks invalid, many guns may bear proof marks which are still perfectly valid but impressed under the Rules of Proof of 1954, 1925 or even earlier. The majority of guns in use today have been proved or reproved since 1925. If in any doubt about the proof condition or status of any weapon it is a good practice to consult a qualified gunmaker. A list of the main Scottish gunmakers appears at the end of Chapter 4.

An important point that should be noted by overseas shooting visitors to Scotland is that in order to purchase cartridges it is essential for the visitor's gun permit to be produced. Similarly, British residents must produce their shotgun certificate. One rather strange provision of the relatively new firearms legislation is that it is no longer possible for foreign nationals to purchase a gun in the UK, use it here and travel home with it. Guns may be bought here by non-British residents but the arms cannot be released to the purchaser and must be exported by the gun dealer direct to the visitor's home address. This is very unfair and frustrating for visitors, particularly if they wish to purchase a quality British gun in the UK and use it whilst they are here. An additional annoyance is that, in many cases, the export procedure will attract an additional import tax in the visitor's home country.

The bewildering array of cartridges that are on offer at most gunshops need cause no confusion. There is no necessity in any form of Scottish gameshooting to use any heavier than the standard 2½ in load of $1\frac{1}{16}$ oz. The lighter 1 oz load is also excellent for all forms of game and it is particularly well suited to the quality lightweight British gun. This load is very light on recoil and is particularly useful for large bag driven pheasant or grouse days or in any form of shooting where large numbers of cartridges are fired. It is a boon for those who are subject to gun headaches. It is often imagined by those who do not really understand ballistics that these popular standard loads are in some way inferior to the considerably more expensive heavy loads. What is not fully appreciated is that these loads are popular simply because they have proved to be the most effective for gameshooting in the UK. Standard load cartridges throw high quality patterns at all normal ranges. It is a good even pattern that makes a cartridge most effective and many of the ultra-heavy loads are inclined to throw somewhat erratic patterns even though they may throw them a little bit further and faster. Heavy load 2¾ and 3 in cartridges are really designed for wildfowling where shots are likely to be taken at tough birds at long range. Such loads should have no place on the general gameshooting scene. The occasional visiting shooter, thinking he will gain some advantage on high pheasants by blasting 2¾ in shells at them, usually ends up after the first drive with a blinding headache and is unable to hit anything or even speak coherently for the rest of the day. During the drive his Scottish neighbour was happily dropping some very high left and rights with his Eley Impax and never had gun headache in his life.

There is an additional advantage of using standard loads as they are readily obtainable throughout the country and, as well as the specialist gunshops, most ironmongers in country towns will carry some stocks. Difficulty sometimes arises for the user of the smaller bore shotgun. Of the gauges other than 12 the least difficult to obtain is the 20 bore, but 16 and 28 bore are often very hard to find even in a gunshop. Some sporting agencies and large shoots will supply clients with cartridges but plenty of advance warning should be given particularly if sizes other than 12 bore are required.

For those who are unfamiliar with the technicalities of guns and cartridges the subject of which shot size to use often causes a great deal of confusion. There are 16 sizes of shot produced by Eley, the main British ammunition maker. These are known in decreasing order of size as single ball, LG, SG, Special SG, SSG, AAA, BB, numbers 1, 3, 4, 5, 6, 7, 8, and 9, plus dust shot. Of these shot sizes only BB, 1, 3, 4, 5, 6, 7, and 8 are used to any extent in wildfowling and gameshooting in the UK.

The problem of what size to use in Scotland is easily resolved. For all forms of game the shooter will be adequately covered if nothing else but no 7 shot is used. A few refinements could be added such as the use of no 6 for very high, late season pheasants and high duck. For specific use on brown or white hare driven shoots, no 4 or 5 shot would generally produce cleaner kills. When solely shooting geese a good shot size to use is no 3. (Specialist guns and loads for wildfowl are discussed in Chapter 11.)

Just as newcomers to the sport are often under the impression that heavy loads are more effective, they may also believe that the larger shot sizes will somehow magically extend the lethal range of their guns. This is a totally erroneous view as it is a good evenly distributed pattern of shot that will consistently hit and kill the game cleanly. With shot sizes 4 and upwards the pattern at 40 yd (37 m) begins to get a bit thin, leaving many gaps through which normal-sized game could pass or, worse, be struck with only one or two pellets thereby causing a wounded bird. The larger shot sizes are appropriate only on large and heavy boned quarry such as geese and hares. If one wishes to be pedantic about shot sizes the following table indicates widely accepted suitable shot sizes for each main species of quarry:

Pheasant 5/6/7	Woodcock 7	Snipe 8
Partridge 6/7	Mallard 5/6/7	Geese BB/1/3
Grouse 6/7	Hare 4/5/6	Teal 6/7
Pigeon 6/7	Rabbit 5/6	Wigeon 6/7

The effective killing range of a shotgun does seem to cause some confusion among inexperienced shooters. In practice it would seem that many appear to be under the impression that the weapon which they are using is a rifle rather than a smoothbore shotgun. These characters may start out by taking shots at distances where, even were they to place a few pellets on target, the possibility of killing the quarry is non–existent. There is of course every possibility that game may be wounded by excessive range shooting and therefore such malpractice is unforgivable and should be speedily brought to a halt by the shoot manager. It should be a personal discipline among any one who pursues game with a gun that shots should never be taken at over 40 yd (37 m). This is the maximum effective range of a 12 bore and smaller bore guns will have a correspondingly lower maximum effective range.

Although smaller bores such as the 20 will propel their pellets as far as will a 12 bore, there will be a reduction in the number of pellets in the pattern and thus their effective range is reduced. It is very unsporting and generally ineffective to shoot at geese at ranges beyond 30 yd (28 m). These recommended maximum ranges sound at first to be incredibly close but it should be noted that the average height of a large mature tree is below 15 yd (14 m). Most shooting of game is done at around treetop height and although appearances are deceptive there are few birds on a driven shoot which are actually out of effective range as they come over the guns. The largest occurrence of out of range shooting takes place on walked up shoots and when gooseshooting. Particular care should be taken not to underestimate range when shooting hares and rabbits, and wildfowlers should not yield to the temptation of employing 'elastic barrels' when shooting at geese. Because of the size and sound of this species as they approach it is very easy to imagine that they are closer than they actually are. Geese are very tough birds and need to be shot well within range and well out in front in order to ensure a clean kill.

BIRTHPLACE OF many a peerless Dickson Round Action. The workshop of famous Scottish gunmakers John Dickson and Sons of Edinburgh in the early 1900s. (*David McKay Brown*)

4 Arms, Ammunition and Equipment for the Rifle Shot

STALKING RIFLES AND CARTRIDGES FOR DEER

THERE ARE SEVERAL factors which must be taken into account when choosing a stalking rifle for use on deer in Scotland. There is an element of choice in some of the aspects which relate to selection of a weapon but one area in which there is no room for argument or debate is that which is laid down by law. Rather curiously, within the UK there are relatively minor differences between Scotland and England on points of law relating to deer seasons, together with the weapons and ammunition used in their pursuit.

In choosing a weapon for stalking in Scotland it is necessary first to decide upon the cartridge to be used from the good range available which meet the legal specifications. In Scotland the law requires the following criteria to be met in a rifle cartridge intended for use on all species of deer *other than roe*. Bullet weight should be not less than 100 grains, muzzle velocity not less than 2,450 ft per second, and muzzle energy not less than 1,750 ft lb. In addition the bullet must be an expanding type, either soft or hollow-nosed.

Suitable cartridges which fall into this category are the .243 Winchester (except with 80 grain bullet), .270 Winchester, .308 Winchester, plus that longstanding Scottish favourite the .275 or 7 mm Mauser as it is commonly known. These are the most widely used calibres in Scotland for red deer stalking, with the .243 and .270 coming at the top of the popularity stakes, but there are several other suitable and legal cartridges which may be employed. The 7 mm Remington Magnum, .275 Rigby, .257 Weatherby Magnum, .257 Roberts, and the famous old .30/06 Springfield (except when using the 220 grain bullet which is just too slow in muzzle velocity), are all eminently suitable, and a visiting sportsman from overseas may already possess a rifle in one of these calibres and be able to arrange to bring it with him. Although roe may be legally shot with weapons of lesser power than those just specified, it is quite legal, if not altogether suitable with some of the heavier calibres, to use any of the above when roe stalking.

The Deer (Firearms) (Scotland) Order 1985 stipulates certain technical specifications for rifles which are to be used on roe deer: bullet weight should be not less than 50 grains, muzzle velocity not less than 2,450 ft per

second, and muzzle energy not less than 1,000 ft lb. Therefore in Scotland it is legal to use the .222 Remington, the .223 Remington, the .220 Swift and the .224 Weatherby Magnum. The first two cartridges in particular are perfect for roe stalking, but all four would be illegal for use against red, fallow or sika deer. If the visitor wishes to have one rifle that will fulfil the role of a sound general purpose weapon for all deer species in Scotland the .243 Winchester would be an excellent choice, provided that the 80 grain bullet was used for no species other than roe. Before the comparatively recent legislation, a most popular calibre roe rifle was the .22 Hornet, but it is now illegal to use this deadly little centre-fire against deer.

The situation in England and Wales is rather different, in that no rifle of a calibre less than .240 or a muzzle energy of less than 1,700 ft lb may be used against any species of deer.

In the bad old days when roe deer were looked upon as a pest and as public enemy number one for the forester, it was legal to use shotguns upon deer and much appalling carnage and wounding was perpetrated during the infamous deer drives. Thankfully the law has now prohibited the use of the shotgun on deer except under certain circumstances by the occupier of enclosed or arable land where deer are claimed to be doing serious damage to crops. If a shotgun is used in these circumstances – and many would question why such a barbarous means of dispatching deer is still permissible – certain specifications are laid down. The shotgun must have a bore of no less than 12 and cartridges used must be loaded with a single rifled slug (which, admittedly, would lay a rhinoceros low if it could hit it!) or the erratic and shockingly nasty SSG or larger shot. Such a concession in the law does permit some shocking acts of cruelty to be performed on our native deer in the name of crop protection. This is a sad situation for a nation that prides itself on its sporting standards and humane treatment of animals. No sportsman worthy of the name would ever consider using a shotgun on deer in any circumstances.

The modern stalker has a wide choice of calibres of sporting rifle but the relatively recent legislation the Deer (Firearms) (Scotland) Order 1985 does prohibit him from using the favourite old-time traditional light-weight rifle the 6.5 mm Mannlicher Schoenauer which does not have the muzzle velocity to meet present-day legal requirements. Many owners of such weapons, with their beautiful German-engineered actions, are having them rebarrelled and chambered for the .243 Winchester cartridge. Similarly, the rifle that won the West and was the meal ticket for many thousands of pioneer Americans, the good old Winchester .30/30, is

not legal for use in Scotland against red deer when using the standard 150 grain bullet, as this is just too slow in muzzle velocity. Winchester produced over a million examples of this famous old .300 calibre lever-action carbine as it was the ideal arm for the horseman, being short in length and easily carried in a saddle holster. With its robust, reliable, fast repeating action and compact 'brush bucking' efficient cartridge it was ideal for hunting deer in the thick brush, as well as keeping the Sioux in their place. One of the penalties to be paid for using the modern ultra-high-velocity rifle cartridge loaded with a relatively light bullet is that should the bullet strike any vegetation during its travel this is likely to cause bullet disintegration or deflection. Therefore great care must be taken to ensure a clear bullet path when stalking in woodland. Some stalkers who are responsible for deer control in large plantations have found that the old western .30/30 rifle is the ideal weapon for them as the bullet's relatively slow velocity enables it to plough through leaves and twigs with impunity and the short carbine is easy to swing on to a running deer and easy to take repeat shots with.

Such methods are rather beyond the normal orbit of deerstalking in Scotland. The greater majority of red deer are shot on the open hill and in general it is not advisable and indeed it is unsporting to advocate shooting at a running beast. The only acceptable time when this may take place is when a beast has been wounded and is making its escape, then every possible effort should be made to dispatch it. The whole point and sport of stalking Scottish red

deer is to approach unseen within a range where, with an accurately placed shot, a certain kill on an undisturbed beast is assured. As the normal shot at red deer on the hill is taken from a solid prone position, with adequate time to take a precisely aimed shot, the type of rifle in general use is as near perfectly adapted to this purpose as possible. Perforce, the result has to be somewhat of a compromise. For instance, in order to achieve maximum accuracy, as in a target rifle, the weapon would require to be so heavy that it would not be practical to transport it over deer terrain. In addition to the essential quality of reasonable accuracy and flat bullet trajectory the stalking rifle must be foolproof, reliable, capable of firing repeat shots quickly, be suited to the fitting of a telescopic sight, be easily operated from a prone position and have an acceptance recoil that will not cause the shooter to flinch every time he squeezes the trigger. A desirable factor for most stalkers is that both rifle and ammunition should be readily available at realistic prices.

The bolt-action Mauser-type rifle most readily meets these criteria. Therefore this is by far the most widely used type of rifle action for Scottish stalking and is what a visiting stalker would be well advised to acquire. The bolt action is one of the most inherently accurate of rifle actions, it is robust, easily maintained and capable of speedy repeat firing. When lying prone and taking a shot it is a simple matter to work the bolt, ejecting the fired round and introducing a fresh round into the chamber, without moving the left hand which is normally resting firmly on a support.

It is available in a vast range of calibres, chambered for every possible design of rimless cartridge, and it is easily fitted with a telescopic sight. It has a positive form of safety catch and the added safety advantage that it is easily demonstrated to be unloaded.

Among other additional types of rifle action which merit some consideration is the single-shot falling block weapon. Such a piece may well attract the stalker who would prefer something that carries the aura of a bygone age but has all the advantages of an ultra modern calibre. Happily such weapons are still made in Scotland, some very fine examples being produced by the Dan'l Fraser Company of Cromarty. This type of action is but rarely seen, and it has all the virtues of the bolt-action except that it does not have the speed in discharging a second or subsequent shot. In a perfect world this would never be necessary, but in practice is a facility which is sometimes required, and when it is speed is of the essence. Only in very skilled hands does the falling block rifle come near the bolt-action in rapidity of fire and its speed is dependent on having cartridges immediately to hand for reloading. None the less these weapons are usually superb examples of the riflemaker's art and there is no real reason why they should not be employed on the hill. With single shot rifles there is perhaps a psychological encouragement for the stalker to take time over a well-placed initial shot which is, after all, the main humane requirement.

If a stalker wishes to be a little extrovert and would like to have a rifle that has its pedigree firmly ensconced among the legends and folk-lore of the far West, he may well fall in love with the evocative lever-action. There is no real technical reason why his fantasies should not be allowed full rein and it is undeniably slightly faster to reload with a lever-action than with the traditional bolt-action. Levers require two simple movements, bolt-actions require four which are more complex. There is no problem in fitting a telescopic sight to a lever-action as the reloading lever drops down and clear of the action body and the spent cases eject from the side of the receiver. One of the drawbacks is that there is not a wide choice of calibres and cartridges as the action requires the cartridge to be of a rimmed type and the range of these is limited. As described earlier, if the weapon is chosen in a calibre which fully meets the legal criteria it will prove adequate if unusual on the hill. With a heavy bullet the lever-action is eminently well-suited to the pursuit of big stags from the deep woodlands.

Even were it possible to say but one thing in favour of the semi-automatic centre-fire rifle for stalking purposes in Scotland its consideration would in any event be purely academic. The Firearms (Amendment) Act 1988 has rendered their use illegal in this country and the same happy fate has befallen the pump-action centre-fire. Not too many tears will have been caused among serious stalkers by such a ban.

In colonial days of yore the English sahib subdued wildlife and sometimes natives with superb British-made side-by-side double rifles. Any eager young administrator journeying forth to serve the white Raj in India or outward-bound for the privileged life in East Africa would be considered ill-equipped were he not to have among his luggage a fine leather case containing a double .350 Rigby-Magnum or similar. Double rifles were in fairly common use on Scottish deer forests up until the First World War, yet despite the fact that these superb sporting arms have the fastest second shot capability of all sporting rifles, they were quickly superseded by the bolt-action. Double rifles are certainly comparatively expensive, built as they are to the standard of a 'best' British shotgun. The change was probably influenced by this cost factor as well as returning servicemen's experience of the rather superior weapons of Mauser design that were issued to Kaiser Bill's team. Today a few notable eccentrics still use a double rifle for stags but, this apart, sadly their use in Scottish sport has now passed into history.

RIFLE SIGHTS

For all forms of Scottish deerstalking the almost universally adopted type of sight is the telescopic. In the Victorian period, when the art of deerstalking as we know it today was rapidly gaining in popularity, iron sights were in common use. The rifles of the day were not particularly accurate and therefore precision aiming devices were somewhat irrelevant. At the time the basic ploy of the stalker was to achieve a position from which he might discharge his piece, thus propelling a large piece of lead at the beast with the principal hope of sufficiently incapacitating it to allow it to be readily seized upon by his accompanying deerhounds. Many a desperate tooth and claw battle would then ensue, with the stalker often entering into the spirit of the thing by hurling boulders at the poor beast's head and finally setting about it with his dirk to administer the *coup de grâce*.

Against this background of mayhem and mishap how astonishing it was that the new-fangled telescopic sight for rifles should be considered unsporting – a perfect example of typical Victorian hypocrisy. British gun and rifle makers of the time were responding energetically to the developing interest in the sport of deerstalking and it was not long before they began to produce rifles which actually did put the bullet where it was supposed to go. The German and Austrian makers were rather ahead of the British in sporting rifle design and their superb weapons cornered a fairly large slice of the British market. Optical engineering began to develop in Germany and it was not long before some excellent quality rifle telescopes began to appear in this country. As rifles became more accurate the need grew for a sighting instrument that was more precise than the open or peep sights in order to utilise fully the inherent capability of the new designs of rifle and high velocity cartridge. Against a surprising amount of opposition from the 'old school' of deerstalking, the telescope soon became acknowledged as the most effective type of rifle sight for Scottish conditions.

One of the main objections to the telescope was that it was thought to make aiming a rifle too easy by optically increasing the size of the target and enabling longer shots to be taken. This was not its prime purpose. Although the rifle 'scope certainly does magnify the target, its main advantage is that it enables the eye to focus on the sight picture in one plane. Iron sights require the eye to attempt to focus on three items at different distances from the eye in the case of open sights, and two items in the case of peep sights. The eye is incapable of doing this and therefore a less precise aiming picture is perceived than with a telescopic sight. Thus with the use of an optical instrument a considerably more precise placing of the bullet is possible. The telescopic sight undoubtedly leads to more humane shooting.

Open sights are comprised of a blade or bead at the muzzle which must be lined up with a V or U-shaped notch in the rear sight which is fitted as far back on the rifle barrel as the action will allow. They do have the advantage of being very cheap and robust, being not easily damaged or knocked off zero and may be used with impunity in heavy rain or damp conditions which would lead to the 'fogging' of an optical sight. It is possible to take an extremely fast sight on a target using open sights. These allow the eye readily to absorb the picture surrounding the target, thus making the stalker aware of other beasts which might be accidentally struck by the bullet passing clean through the target animal. In many ways open sights are well suited to the stalker who pursues his deer in heavy wood-land and who may often require to take a very speedy shot in an obscured situation.

Aperture or 'peep' sights differ from open sights in that the rear sight is comprised of a very small hole at the end of a folding leg which is fixed at the rear of the rifle's action and therefore very close to the shooter's eye. When sighting on a target the eye is forced to look through this small aperture and automatically lines it up with the fore sight so that the eye has then to focus only on fore sight and target. Like the telescopic sight, 'peep' sights do have the disadvantage that it is not easy to pick up the target in the aperture or viewing field quickly. The aperture is the type of sight in common use for target rifle competitions and although it is effective as a sporting sight in skilled hands, it has little place in modern-day stalking.

Even for those who are blessed with perfect eyesight there is little argument to support the use of any type of rifle sight other than the telescopic for the vast majority of deerstalking situations in Scotland. The sport of deer-stalking should be based on the challenge of approaching an animal close enough to make certain of a clean kill. The telescopic sight should never be used to short-cut this process.

Deerstalking should have nothing to do with demonstrations of long distance target shooting. Those who wish to use a rifle for this purpose should confine their activities to the ranges at Bisley and not practise them in the deer forest. The legitimate use of the telescopic sight is as a humane aid to precision bullet placement. In addition to its advantages of single plane focusing and magnification of the target, one big advantage that the optical sight offers is its considerable light-gathering power. In dull light conditions, a 'scope with a fairly low magnification and a large object glass will illuminate the target and its surroundings to an astonishing degree. Such a facility is invaluable to late evening roe and sika stalkers and many a beast owes its death in the dusk to this feature.

Rather surprisingly, the British optical industry has always let itself be beaten in the production of high quality sporting optical instruments, and Germany continues to produce among the very finest binoculars and rifle telescopes in the world. The renowned names of Zeiss, Pecar, Optikon, Ajak, Habicht and Kahles all spring readily to mind. All these companies produce a range of high quality sights which, as well as being optically excellent, are robustly made, many of them having metal tubes. Such high quality items do cost rather a lot of money, in some cases as much as a quality rifle, but a purchase is likely to form a lifetime investment. As in the production of so many other items, the Japanese have for some time given the Germans some stiff competition in optical goods. Japanese rifle 'scopes may not be as strongly made or have the lasting qualities of the German telescopes, being for the main part built on plastic tubes, but they are of adequate quality, some with very good optics, and they offer excellent value for money. Because of the widespread use of sporting rifles in the United States and Canada there are some excellent instruments available from across the Atlantic, some of which are equal to the best that Germany produces.

When choosing a rifle telescope it is easy for the novice to be confused by the varying technical descriptions. Rifle telescope specification is given as two figures, the first being the degree of magnification indicated by a figure followed by an X and the second figure representing the diameter of the object glass (the furthest lens from the eye), eg, 4X90, 6X40 etc. These are known as four by ninety, six by forty etc. It is particularly desirable, for those who expect much of their stalking to take place in bad light, to acquire a 'scope with the largest practicable and afford-able object lens. The larger this lens is, the more light-gathering power it will have and thus the more illuminated will be the sight picture, a factor which could make all the difference in securing a trophy at last light. Even during the day good light-gathering power is an advantage in dull conditions. Rifle 'scopes with a large object glass are consider-ably more expensive, but for the stalker who can make good use of their additional illumination, they are a very worthwhile investment.

The beginner may naturally be tempted in the direction of a high power 'scope, thinking that this may well confer some real advantage, and the attraction of a variable power is under-standable. High power 'scopes originate in the main from the United States, largely because ulta-long-range shooting is more often practised there; 'varmint' shooting at 1,000 yd and pronghorn antelope at 500 yd is a style of shooting quite common. This has encouraged the development of rifle 'scopes with very high magnifications of up to 20X. To the novice it may sound a wonderful idea to magnify his target 20 times, but he has only to try to line up on a stag with a 'scope like this to realise how difficult it is to locate a target quickly through the extremely limited field of view possessed by these powerful 'scopes. As well as magnifying the target the telescope also magnifies the natural shake of the rifleman and with an ultra-high power this may be most disconcerting. Such 'scopes are almost useless in bad light. Variable power 'scopes are not a good idea for general deerstalking as they are more subject to damage and to being knocked off zero. They give the stalker yet one more unnecessary technical detail to be concerned with, providing little if any real advantage, and a variable power will cost a deal of unnecessary extra cash. The purchase of a telescope with a large object glass would be a better buy.

A four power 'scope would be the best compromise for all-round Scottish deerstalking and if the rifleman feels compelled to have something more powerful then he should certainly go no higher than a six power.

One other choice which requires to be made when selecting a rifle 'scope is the style of reticle to be employed. The reticle is the sighting device within the telescope. The simplest form is the cross-hair, which has the point of aim precisely where the hairs inter-sect. There is a range of alternatives from thick posts, either flat topped or pointed, dotted lines and various combinations of all of these. For roe and sika stalking, where shots may often be taken in woodland or bad light, some form of easily seen post reticle is an aid. A good all-round combination design is the basic cross-hair which has the outer lines formed thick and black, sharply tapering to fine cross-hairs in the centre. This allows a very quick placing of the general target picture and a final ultra-precise placement of the point of aim. On the whole, reticles are largely a matter of personal choice and there is no completely incorrect style for any given purpose.

There seems to be a current vogue in some quarters for having a small, two-legged, collapsible stand attached to the rifle fore-end to provide a solid rest for shooting from the prone position. Such devices do give some additional advantage on occasions where there is plenty of time to set up for the shot and they do permit more accurate shooting at extreme range. The drawback is that they are an unnecessary technical accessory to be concerned with, requiring time to adjust. In addition, they do have an irritating tendency to get caught up in heather just at the wrong moment, making it difficult to slide the rifle smoothly over a knoll as the stalker eases up to take the shot. Apart from other considerations they do give a rather 'Rambo-style' military appearance to the stalker. These mini-bipods provide a useful accessory for the long range 'varmint' or fox shooter, but are not recommended for normal deerstalking.

THE STALKER'S GLASS

A visitor could have a perfectly enjoyable and successful stalking trip to Scotland whilst possessing no specialist equipment of his own other than a pair of boots and the clothes on his back. Most estates will provide a rifle and ammunition for the visiting sportsman if required. However, in addition to acquiring his own rifle, there are several other items which, no doubt, he will wish to have eventually and which could add enormously to his enjoyment.

A 'glass' of his very own will open up a whole new aspect of the sport, allowing him to take an active part in the whole process. Apart from the initial locating of deer – and even on the open hill they are astonishingly difficult for the inexperienced eye to spot – detailed assessment of beasts is impossible without some form of optical aid. The professional stalker invariably uses a telescope, and this requires some considerable skill and experience. The stalker is well used to spotting deer with the naked eye but requires the high magnification of the telescope to examine the beasts in fine detail. A stalking telescope will have a magnification of 20X or 30X. With the telescope it is necessary to use a stick or other form of support in order to overcome the user's natural shake, as these instruments are extremely difficult to hold sufficiently steady in a freestanding position. They do have the added advantage of being extremely portable and the traditional type folds neatly away into an easily carried leather case.

Although to achieve the full potential of the telescope requires some considerable practice, it is an art worth acquiring. If the tyro stalker anticipates that he will take up the sport on a regular basis he should feel encouraged to acquire a good stalking glass and practise its use. He will gain a very great deal once he develops the skill fully. The Ross three-draw brass telescope was and still is the most popular stalking glass in Scotland. In its neat purpose-built leather case complete with sling, this is a very easy instrument to carry and may be brought into use very rapidly. Sadly the good old Ross 'scope has not been manufac-

tured for some years, but they are virtually everlasting and many hundreds are still in everyday use on the hill. Well-conditioned examples command very respectable prices and are beginning to acquire a collectable status. There has been a long period when telescopes of this style were unavailable, but happily the position has now changed and a traditional Scottish-style stalking telescope can be supplied by Gray & Co, 23, Harbour Road, Inverness. IV1 1UF (tel: 0463 233225). This three-draw telescope is made from lightweight alloy with bloomed lenses of high optical performance and is supplied in the customary blocked hide case, baize lined with leather shoulder sling.

The occasional visiting stalker may well be better served by a pair of binoculars as they are much easier to use and will also be useful for a number of other purposes. Practically any pair of binoculars will be of some assistance on the hill, but if they are to be chosen specifically for stalking it is as well to bear the following points in mind.

As with rifle 'scopes, a really high magnification in a pair of binoculars intended for stalking use is likely to be counter-productive. As the magnification increases the field of view decreases, and the binoculars become more difficult to hold sufficiently steady as the shake in the user's hands is also magnified. The depth of field of binoculars' lenses is very significant – a wide depth of field means that there is a longer distance that will be sharp and in focus between two points in the line of sight thus giving a much clearer picture of the object being viewed and its immediate surroundings. The depth of field also diminishes as the magnification rises. A large diameter object glass will give much improved illumination and light-gathering power but, if this is taken to extremes, the instrument may well become excessively bulky and heavy. Roe stalkers, who are likely to benefit the most from the maximum light gathering power in binoculars, could cope more easily with a heavy and bulky pair with an extra large object glass as they do not normally need to walk so far as red deer-stalkers and seldom have to crawl on their bellies for any distance. Red deer stalkers should bear in mind that their binoculars will have to be hung about their person throughout a long day and for many a weary mile and in the final stages of a stalk they will have to be attached to the crawling body somehow. By halfway through a morning on the hill, the proud owner of a massive pair of magnificent maritime glasses made for a German submarine commander might begin to regard them with as much favour as the Ancient Mariner bestowed on the albatross.

A suitable compromise must obviously be made and a magnification between six and ten times with an object glass of 40 or 50 is recommended for all-round deerstalking use in Scotland. As far as quality and value for money goes, the situation with binoculars is very similar to that mentioned above for rifle 'scopes, although as there is a larger market for binoculars there is an even wider choice available. It is worth bearing in mind that, in red deer stalking in particular, binoculars are inclined to suffer from being exposed to damp, extreme weather conditions and to occasional sudden contact with rocks. Therefore it is an advantage to have a fairly robust pair. A pair of top-quality German binoculars with the finest of lenses is a superb instrument to use on the hill, but many people might grudge subjecting such an expensive item to the sort of rigorous treatment that stalking often involves.

OTHER STALKING AIDS

There is a host of items that a newcomer to the sport of stalking might be persuaded to take with him on the hill. If the tyro stalker has ever attended a course of mountain training at one of the multitude of outdoor centres which seem to have sprung up over-night in many a highland glen, he might feel obliged to transport with him a vast mound of protective clothing and equipment before ever daring to set foot on a Scottish hill. This might range from a survival blanket, a change of socks and underwear, balaclava, gloves, additional waterproof clothing, large packed lunch with thermos flask, torch, compass, map, whistle, sleeping bag, first aid equipment, flares and not forgetting that absolute necessity, without which no trained mountaineer would dare step off a highland road – the redoubtable Kendal Mint Cake. Naturally all this would require a sizeable rucksack, and the amount of energy required to move this load over the hill would severely drain its carrier's resources.

The best basic advice with regard to ancillary equipment for stalking is that if it does not fit in the pocket of your jacket then forget it. Mountain training, as promoted by educational establishments, has naturally to err very much on the side of over precaution and safety. Taking a realistic view, it should be borne in mind that many of these centres are staffed by personnel who were originally city-bred, invariably from south of the border. Seldom do they have the natural inbred intuitive feeling for and deep knowledge of the Scottish terrain and weather possessed by the local stalker. The mountain instructor may be an expert in mountain rescue, survival and the building of snow holes, but the professional stalker makes damn sure that he never puts himself or his client in a position where these techniques are needed. If weather conditions are likely to be dangerous on the hills the highland stalker stays off them.

One item that every deerstalker should carry in his pocket or attached to his person is a knife. This should be suitable for bleeding and gralloching and, should it be necessary, carrying out the unpleasant task of completing the killing of a beast that has been shot but is not quite dead. There are many different styles of knife that will fulfil this purpose such as sheath knives, knives that fit into a pouch worn on the belt and various types of pocket knife. The most popular for Scottish stalking is the folding lock-blade. This has a sharp pointed, slightly curved, single blade of around 4 in (10 cm), sharpened on one side only, which locks firmly into place when opened out from the handle. The handle is rectangular in shape and section which ensures that it does not slip round in the hand when in use. The furnishings of this knife are usually brass and the handle plates of rosewood or staghorn. The 'Rolls-Royce' version is made in Germany and priced accordingly whilst, as is the way of things, adequate copies are available from Japan, China and Pakistan for very modest sums. The wise owner, particularly if he has the German version, will see that his knife has a hole in the handle to accommodate a lanyard with which to attach it to his clothing. Pockets are apt to empty themselves very readily when deerstalking. Most visiting sportsmen will be accompanied by a professional stalker who will almost certainly have a knife and be the one to use it but a spare carried by his rifle is always a good insurance. Roe stalkers are more likely to be out unaccompanied than those who pursue red deer and they should, of course, be equipped and able to deal with the carcase of their quarry by themselves.

A stout rope is a real asset when it comes to dragging a beast for any distance. This is usually carried by the professional but a sportsman out on his own would be well advised to take one with him. The rope, which need not be any longer than 20 ft, (6 m), may be easily carried wound around the waist or across the (non-shooting) shoulder, alpine-style.

A light lunch tucked into the jacket pocket will keep the hunger pangs away for most of the day. The serious deerstalker must forget a flask of coffee and alcohol, as it is too cumbersome. One thing of which there is no lack in a Scottish deer forest is the means to slake a thirst. There is always plenty of ice-cold water around – the finest in the world.

One aid that is well worth taking on the hill is a good stick. Young and agile may scoff at such a suggestion, but a hill-stick should in no way be regarded as something solely for the aged and infirm. A stick is a great help in keeping one's balance and acts as a third leg when traversing rough ground, steep slopes, hill burns and other hazards. It is almost essential as a rest when using a telescope and helps greatly to steady binoculars. Woodland stalkers may find a stick to be invaluable as a rifle rest when obliged to take a standing shot. When dragging a deer carcas, if the rope is wound around the shaft of the stick, this will greatly ease the pressure on the hands. Most sticks seen in Scotland are made from hazel, ash or the more exotic blackthorn and it is wise to avoid those which are metal-tipped. The life of many a stag has been saved by the clink of a metal-shod stick on rock. A stout rubber ferrule is a better proposition.

It is an age-old custom for Scottish countrymen to while away the long winter nights by producing horn-handled sticks for the hill. The handle is fashioned from the horn of a blackface ram and the method of treating the horn and forming it into handles of the most exquisitely crafted designs is a well-guarded secret. Stickmaking has developed into an artform in its own right and is true Scottish craftmanship as it should be, where the object is both a work of art and a truly functional and useful item. The ram's horn handles may be carved into a great variety of shapes with the most popular design incorporating the national emblem – the thistle. Such a stick, in addition to being very

useful, would make a wonderful memento of a Scottish sporting holiday and a very up-market conversation piece when casually placed in the hall or den at home.

Clothing for deerstalking is an important topic and this is discussed in Chapter 5.

SUPPLIERS OF SPORTING WEAPONS, AMMUNITION AND EQUIPMENT

Most of the undernoted businesses will be able to supply the visiting sportsman's needs in guns, rifles, accessories and ammunition.

Aberdeenshire and Kincardineshire

Anderson Guns, 201, Hardgate, Aberdeen, AB1 2YP. Tel: 0224 201179.
Wm Brown & Co, 11, Belmont Street, Aberdeen. Tel: 0224 641692.
Countrywear, 35, Bridge Street, Ballater. Tel: 0338 55453.
George Manson, 45, Gordon Street, Huntly. Tel: 0466 2482.
Murray's Gunshop, 4, Bridge Street, Banchory, AB3 3FR. Tel: 03302 4319.
Robertson Sports, 1/3, Kirk Street, Peterhead.
Sloan International Ltd, 125–129, High Street, Inverurie, AB5 9QJ. Tel: 0467 25181.
George Smith & Co, 15, Bridge Street, Ballater. Tel: 0338 55432.

Angus

Fishing Tackle & Guns, 180, High Street, Montrose. Tel: 0674 72692.

W R Hardy (Gunsmith), 153, East High Street, Forfar. Tel: 0307 66635.
Stephen's Tackle & Guns, 22, Bank Street, Kirriemuir. Tel: 0575 72378.

Ayrshire

Allsports, 7/5, The Square, Cumnock, KA18 1BJ. Tel: 0290 25002.
Fair Game, 5, Chalmers Arcade, Girvan, KA26 9ES. Tel: 0465 4094.
Gamesport (Ayr) Ltd, 60, Sandgate, Ayr, KA7 1BX. Tel: 0292 263822.
James Kirk, Burn's Statue Square, Ayr. Tel: 0292 263390.
McCririck & Sons, 38, John Finnie Street, Kilmarnock. Tel: 0563 25577.

Berwickshire, Roxburghshire & Peebles-shire

The Country Gunshop, Lilliesheaf, Melrose, TD6 9JD. Tel: 083 57315.
John Dickson & Son, 35, The Square, Kelso. Tel: 0573 24687.
Ian Fraser Sports, 1, Bridgegate, Peebles. Tel: 0721 20979.
Mackenzie's All Sports, 76, High Street, Coldstream, TD12 4DH. Tel: 0890 2865.
Game & Country Enterprises, 6/8, Canongate, Jedburgh, TD8 6AJ. Tel: 0835 63019.
R Welsh & Son, 28, Castle Street, Duns, TD11 3DP. Tel: 0361 83466.

Caithness

C H Haygarth & Sons, The Cottage Gunshop, Dunnet, KW14 8XQ. Tel: 084785 602.

Wilson & Nolf, 1 Francis Street, Wick, KW1 5PZ. Tel: 0955 4284.

Dumfries, Galloway & Wigtownshire

Castle Douglas Guns & Tackle, 9, St Andrews Street, Castle Douglas. Tel: 0556 2977.
Galloway Guns & Tackle, 36, Arthur Street, Newton Stewart. Tel: 0671 3404.
Gordon Sports, 67, High Street, Lockerbie. Tel: 05762 2400.
M McGowan & Son, 41/43, High Street, Dalbeattie, DG5 4AN.
M McGowan & Son, 50/52, King Street, Castle Douglas, DG7 1AE. Tel: 0556 2009.
Pattie's of Dumfries, 109, Queensberry Street, Dumfries, DG1 1BH. Tel: 0387 52891.
Solway Shooting Supplies, 8, The Green, Eastriggs, Annan.
The Gun Shop, 14, Queen Street, Newton Stewart. Tel: 0671 2570.

Dunbartonshire

Ian Tyrell Guns, 165, High Street, Dumbarton. Tel: 0389 34438.

Dundee

Angus Gun Room, 98 Ferry Road, Dundee. Tel: 0382 453668.
J Gow & Sons, 12, Union Street, Dundee, DD1 4BH. Tel: 0382 25427.
Shotcast Ltd; 8, Whitehall Crescent, Dundee, DD1 4AU. Tel: 0382 25621.

Edinburgh

John Dickson & Son, 21, Frederick Street, Edinburgh, EH2 2NE. Tel: 031 225 4218.
Edinburgh Gunmakers, 73, Rose Street, Edinburgh. Tel: 031 225 2641.
Field & Stream Ltd, 61, Montrose Terrace, Edinburgh, EH7 5DP. Tel: 031 661 4282.
Shooting Lines Ltd, 23, Roseburn Terrace, Edinburgh, EH12 5NG. Tel: 031 337 8616.
F & D Simpson, 28, West Preston Street, Edinburgh, EH8 9PZ.
M B Thomson & Son, 19, East London Street, Edinburgh. Tel: 031 556 5682.

Fife

The Shooting Developments Co (Shooting Accessories/Decoys), Valley Drive, Leslie, KY6 3BQ. Tel: 0592 745029.
Were Game, 126, Clair Street, Kirkcaldy. Tel: 0592 54301.

Morayshire

R M Jeffries, 39, New Street, Rothes. Tel: 0340 3407.
G G Mortimer & Son, 61, High Street, Grantown on Spey. Tel: 0479 2684.

Orkney Islands

Robert H Hall (Guns), Willowburn Road, Kirkwall, KW15 1NE. Tel: 0856 2880.

Perthshire

James Crockart & Sons, 28, Allan Street, Blairgowrie, PH10 6AD. Tel: 0250 2056.

Highland Guns & Tackle, Blair Cottages, Blair Atholl. Tel: 0796 81 303.

M & G Guns & Tackle, 51, York Place, Perth, PH2 8EH. Tel: 0738 25769.

P D Malloch, 259, Old High Street, Perth. Tel: 0738 32316.

A Turner, 85, North Methven Street, Perth. Tel: 0738 23679.

Ross & Cromarty

Dan'l Fraser & Co (Gun & Rifle Makers), Peddieston, Cromarty, IV11 8XX. Tel: 03817 294.

MacLean Sports, 33, High Street, Dingwall. Tel: 0349 63147.

R MacLeod & Son, 14, Lamington Street, Tain. Tel: 0862 2171.

Isle of Skye

The Gun & Tackle Room, Uiginish Lodge, Dunvegan. Tel: 047 022 445.

Shooters Supplies, 4, Luib, Broadford, IV49 9AN. Tel: 047 12 594.

Stirling & Clackmannan

D Crockart & Son, 47, King Street, Stirling. Tel: 0786 73443.

Glasgow Range Supplies Ltd, 6, Main Street, Menstrie. Tel: 0259 61301.

J K Guns, 101, Mary Square, Laurieston, Falkirk. Tel: 0324 23156.

Sutherland

Rob Wilson, Rod & Guns, Brora. Tel: 0408 21373.

Glasgow Area

Crocket Ltd, 136, West Hill Street, Glasgow. Tel: 041 332 1041.

David McKay Brown (Gunmakers) Ltd, 32, Hamilton Road, Bothwell, G17 8NA. Tel: 0698 853727

Glasgow Gunmakers, 14, Hamilton Street, Clydebank, Tel: 041 951 1825.

Guns & Tackle, 25, Portland Place, Hamilton. Tel: 0698 422904.

Pitcher's Sports, 23, Moss Street, Paisley. Tel: 041 8896969.

Tackle & Guns Ltd, 918, Pollockshaws Road, Glasgow, G41 2ET. Tel: 041 632 2733.

Inverness-shire

J Graham & Co Ltd, 71, Castle Street, Inverness. Tel: 0463 233178.

Gray & Co, 23, Harbour Road, Inverness. Tel: 0463 233225.

J Ormiston & Co, Market Brae Steps, Inverness. IV2 3AB. Tel: 0463 222757.

Rod & Gun Shop, 68, High Street, Fort William. Tel: 0397 2656.

Spey Tackle & Guns, 72, High Street, Kingussie, PH21 1HZ. Tel: 0540 661565.

Lothians

Hawthorn Shooting Centre, 78A, High Street, Bonnyrigg. Tel: 031 660 1111.

J S Main & Sons, 87, High Street, Haddington. Tel: 062 082 2148.

WELL FOUND! A tricky retrieve for Tarka, the author's labrador. (*John Andrews*)

5 The Art of Good Gunmanship

GENERAL GUN SAFETY

Never, ever let your gun,
Pointed be at any one.

A TRITE LITTLE homily this, but it does sum up the basic safety procedure which is the most important factor in shooting custom and etiquette. Apart from the general undesirability of shooting a fellow sportsman, it should be fully realised that a host or shooting party organiser is at perfect liberty to insist that a gun who has demonstrated some unsafe behaviour should immediately leave the shooting field. This applies equally whether the gun is a guest or is paying for the privilege to shoot. The following general gun safety points should be noted.

- Always treat every gun or rifle as loaded and therefore potentially dangerous.
- Always check that a gun or rifle is unloaded immediately you handle it.
- Always ensure that the barrels are never pointed at anything that you do not intend to shoot.
- Always pass a shotgun to someone stock first, with the breech open and empty.
- Always carry a shotgun open and empty when in company.
- Never put down a loaded shotgun or rifle.
- Always leave a weapon in such a way that it cannot be knocked over or fall. Remember that dogs are a particular hazard in this respect.
- Never allow children to handle guns or cartridges.
- Never load a weapon indoors.
- Always store weapons and ammunition securely.
- Never travel or enter a vehicle with a loaded weapon.

General Safety in the Shooting Field

- Always carry a shotgun so that it cannot point at anyone. The two acceptable methods are over the crook of the arm with the barrels pointing at the ground, or over the shoulder with the trigger guard uppermost and the barrels never allowed to tilt towards the horizontal.
- Always unload your gun when crossing or negotiating an obstacle, whether in company or alone.
- When in company and requiring to cross a fence or wall the following procedure should be followed:

1 Open guns and remove cartridges.
2 One shooter passes his gun, open and stock first, to his companion.
3 First shooter crosses obstacle and takes both guns from his companion.
4 The second shooter crosses the obstacle and takes back his gun.
5 Reloading may then take place and the shoot be continued.

- When alone and requiring to cross an obstacle, after the gun is unloaded it should be placed where it can not fall over as the shooter negotiates the obstacle.
- After laying a gun on the ground always check to make sure that no stray material has entered the barrels. Even a leaf or piece of mud may cause an obstruction sufficient to cause a burst barrel when the gun is fired. It is particularly important to be aware of this when shooting in snow. It is only too easy to pick up snow in the muzzles which may produce disastrous consequences at the next shot unless cleared.

- Be particularly careful when loading a shotgun to ensure that the muzzles are kept pointing at the ground. The correct procedure is to raise the stock to the barrels in closing the breech.
- Always keep the fingers well clear of the triggers at all times except, of course, when taking a shot.
- Do not rely implicitly on the safety catch. This is a mechanical device and therefore liable to misfunction. The safety catch should not be released until a shot is about to be fired. It should be slipped off during the action of raising the gun to the shoulder. If a shot is not taken it should be ensured that the safety is carefully slipped back on whilst the barrels are pointing either to the ground or the sky.

DRIVEN GROUSE SAFETY AND ETIQUETTE

When shooting driven grouse the beaters will normally walk right up to the butts. The usual procedure is to stop shooting in front as the beaters draw within range. The guns will then turn round and will only shoot at birds once they have passed the butts. This is normally signalled by a blast on a whistle or a toot on a horn from the head keeper. The signal must be implicitly obeyed as must the signal which indicates the finish of the drive and the total ceasefire. Driven grouse shooters must be particularly aware of the position of any pickers-up behind the butts and ensure that they do not receive any unwelcome charges of shot.

Grouse and also partridge are apt to fly fairly close to the ground. When shooting from a grouse butt it is only too easy for an inexperienced gun to swing after approaching birds as they pass through the line of butts. This is about the worst crime that one could commit on the grouse moor and must be prevented at all cost. The result of a gun in the neighbouring butt receiving your charge of shot full in the face at 40 yards would be totally horrific and you would never forgive yourself for the rest of your life. The recipient could very easily be killed or blinded. Apart from other considerations, there is always the possibility of police action for criminal assault and civil action for vast sums in damages. Many grouse butts are fitted with safety markers, which are sticks placed in the sides of the butt to remind guns of the whereabouts of neighbouring butts and physically to prevent guns from swinging through the line. Where these are not fitted to butts extra care must be taken. Try to shoot all birds in front of the butt. If it is necessary to follow birds as they pass through the line of butts in order to have a shot behind, then the gun **must** be removed from the shoulder and the barrels kept vertical as the shooter turns to fire behind the line. It is perfectly in order to shoot at birds overhead provided that they are well up in the air above the line of butts.

It is bad form to shoot at birds which are nearer to your neighbour as these are 'his' birds. Ground game may normally be shot on a driven grouse day provided that shooting is confined to the front and ceases altogether at ground game when the beaters' approach is

signalled by the keeper. On the whole it is perhaps wise to ignore hares and rabbits, as inevitably a good covey will come straight over your head just as you have had two ineffective barrels at an approaching mountain hare.

DRIVEN PHEASANT SAFETY AND ETIQUETTE

Do make sure that you know exactly where the meeting place for the shoot is and arrive in plenty of time.

Go to your stand as quickly and as quietly as you can once you have been so directed by the shoot organiser. Do not carry out loud conversations with neighbours or companions. Pheasants have excellent hearing and are very much averse to the human voice. Talking may well deter game from coming forward.

Do not move from the immediate vicinity of your peg even if it seems that a move will put you in a better spot. Only if the organiser signals you to move is it permissible to do so.

Try to remember the number which you drew at the start of the day and what the arrangement is about moving at each drive. The pegs are usually numbered from the right of the line as it faces the drive. Standard procedure is to move up two numbers at each drive.

It is a good safe policy never to shoot ground game at a driven pheasant shoot even if it has been indicated that this is permissible. If you must have a shot at a hare or rabbit it must be clearly established that you are not endangering fellow guns, beaters, stops, pickers-up or dogs. Far better to concentrate on the pheasants. Never, ever be tempted to fire at any species of deer which may come near during the drive.

Never, ever shoot birds of prey.

Unless you are very experienced at shooting foxes, are aware that the owner and keeper will approve and are absolutely certain of a safe shot and a clean kill, simply raise your hat to any fox that may come by.

Never, ever shoot low birds. They really should be at tree-top height to be considered at all sporting. Be very careful when shooting at drives which have rising or high ground in front of the guns. There may well be times when beaters and stops may be at a considerably higher level than the guns and lowish shots could endanger them. The host or keeper should indicate the presence of any stops who may be in range of your stand but sometimes communications are not all that they should be.

Be aware that there are likely to be pickers-up behind you. The easiest, safest and most sporting policy to adopt is to refuse to take any shot that could possibly be described as unsporting or low. This has the bonus that you will probably find that you will enjoy much more sporting and satisfying shooting in this way.

Always ensure that your gun is unloaded immediately the signal is given for the end of each drive. This is usually made by a horn or whistle. Following the signal, the gun should be placed in its slip, no matter what further opportunities to shoot occur. Your gun should remain in its slip until you are ready to shoot at the next stand.

Obey the final ceasefire signal implicitly, even if the best bird you have ever seen is approaching your stand. He who dares to shoot after the end of drive signal will soon make himself most unpopular.

Some estates have pure white pheasants amongst their stock, which are reasonably easy to spot even in a flush of birds. Do not shoot white birds unless you have specifically been instructed to do so. If you attend an end of season cocks only shoot make sure that you only shoot cocks. Even in silhouette, January cock pheasants are pretty easy to distinguish from hens as their tails and necks are much longer. Shooting hens may cost you £20 each as a fine.

Do not pinch your neighbour's birds. It is the height of bad manners in the shooting field and if there is any doubt about approaching game, call out the traditional 'your bird' to your neighbour. Thus you will soon gain the reputation of being a 'true gentleman and a scholar'.

If you are shooting as a guest it is a pleasant courtesy to write a short note in thanks to your host after the day.

GUNDOG ETIQUETTE AND SAFETY

An acceptable gundog should be completely steady and under control at all times. It should be guaranteed not to chase hares and rabbits or domestic and farm animals. It should not run in to the fall of the game and should not retrieve until instructed to do so. It should not be prone to poach another dog's retrieve. It should sit quietly whilst a drive is underway and should not whine or bark. It should not jump up at people, leaving muddy footprints on expensive shooting suits. It should be soft-mouthed and retrieve game tenderly and in an undamaged condition. It should not eat game, although the handler should ensure that hungry dogs and game are not left in the same transport together. Even if your dog is not a perfect retriever or finder and flusher of game, if it has none of the aforementioned vices it will be accepted on any shoot. If it is subject to committing any of the misdemeanours listed leave it at home. An ill-trained dog will ruin its owner's day as well as making him highly unpopular.

Never attach a dog to yourself whilst shooting. If the animal needs that sort of discipline it is not fit for the shooting field.

When shooting over dogs, obviously the guns must take great care to ensure that they do not take any extra-low shot which might endanger the dogs. Ground game presents a particular hazard in this respect – even the best of field trial dogs occasionally forgets itself under extreme temptation and may have a short pursuit of a hare or rabbit flushed under its nose. The shooter, concentrating on the game, may not notice the hot-foot spaniel behind it and if he is prone to shooting behind his carelessness may be a very expensive mistake. Apart from the obvious humanitarian concerns, good working gundogs are very valuable and may be worth well over £1,000. Griefstricken and irate owners of dead dogs are not the easiest of people to apologise to.

Most formal driven shoots will have the

NANCY MCNICOL with Panda, a brilliant English setter. (*Roger Ridman*)

assistance of several pickers-up. The main job of these helpers is to retrieve and humanely dispatch wounded game as soon as possible and to find game which falls into heavy cover, into water or out of sight. Most will have a brace or more of dogs, usually labradors or golden retrievers, and they will be stationed at a place which gives them a decent view at some distance behind the line of guns. Therefore it is very important, when driven pheasant shooting in particular, not to take low shots at any time, either in front or behind.

It is very helpful if each gun keeps a mental tally of the numbers and approximate whereabouts of each bird shot during a drive and to liaise with the nearest picker-up at the close of each drive. Do not expect each picker-up to have precisely noted each bird that you shoot. It may be that he/she had to set off after a strong runner or two during the course of the drive and may not have been in a position to view everything. Do not expect a handler to have his dogs retrieve every bird that you have shot which is lying in the open in clear view. Such retrieves are detrimental to the true work of a gundog and guns should not be above at least collecting such game together, which they may then leave at their pin. If they wish to show a little extra consideration, it is always appreciated if they could carry some of their birds back to the gamecart themselves.

If you have a decent well-trained dog which accompanies you to a formal shoot, you may wish to give it as many retrieves as possible. The handlers will not mind in the least, as long as your dog is efficient, but they do prefer to be advised of your wishes beforehand.

However, do be aware that no picker-up worth his/her salt will ever leave a definite 'runner' until after the drive and you may expect immediate efforts to be made to collect and dispatch such birds without delay.

'Runners' are birds that have been dropped but which may have just a damaged wing or other non-fatal wound. Unfortunately these do occur on occasion, and such birds often crash down and then take to their heels at great speed. Do not ever be tempted to finish off such a bird by shooting it on the ground. Although this may seem expedient, it is an action fraught with danger and is very bad form indeed. Dogs and humans may be endangered by such action and the correct remedy is to draw the attention of a picker-up to the situation as soon as possible.

TIPPING AND GRATUITIES

This is an area which does cause a deal of embarrassment to visitors who are unfamiliar with the British formal shooting scene. The practice of tipping gamekeepers and stalkers originated in the days before commercial shooting, when all the guns would be free guests of the landowner. Landowners have never been renowned for overpaying their staff, and crafty hosts would encourage their shooting guests to drop a coin or two into the hand of the keeper at the end of the day. With this as an established practice, the owner could then happily regard such payments as a legitimate addition to the keeper's basic and poor wage. This helped the laird's coffers and his conscience. It would soon come to his ears

if a guest had sloped off without the customary gratuity-laden handshake to the keeper. Such a guest would not readily be invited again.

Tipping is still very much an accepted custom on any shoot where a keeper is involved. Some paying guns on commercial shoots may resent parting with additional cash for their sport at the end of the day. Perhaps they should pause a little to consider the facts.

Most gamekeepers still exist and rear their families on what is the very modest basic agricultural wage. Few keepers are in the job solely for the money that they can make from it. Most are there because, for them, it is a way of life and a job that they love. If you were to total up the hours that the average keeper puts in every week, his wages would seem very low. Certainly most of the profession are supplied with free housing and other perks but this seldom amounts to a high standard of living. Most keepers will be responsible for around ten shoots per year and these are the only occasions when he has a chance to make any significant addition to his basic wage.

If you have enjoyed a good day's sport this will be very largely due to the keeper's efforts. It is a rather pleasant custom if the gun shows his appreciation by distributing a little largesse. The traditional time for the tip to be conveyed on a shoot where the gun is staying overnight is in the gun room at the end of the day if the keeper is cleaning the guests' gun. A few short words of appreciation mean a great deal to most of this hardworking breed and probably just as much as the few pound notes which should accompany the interchange. The other traditional time for this little ceremony is when the keeper presents each gun with the customary brace of game. Old experienced shooting men are a joy to watch in this situation, where the art is not to draw attention to the vulgar exchange of cash. The sleight of hand employed by these old boys in its transfer would do credit to a conjurer.

How much to give is always a problem. At 1991 prices, on any driven day where the total bag exceeds 200 head, then a £20 tip from each gun would be the standard expectation. For every 100 head increase in the bag the tip should be enlarged by at least £5 but preferably by £10. On a walking or wildfowling day, £10 to the keeper per gun would be normal, regardless of the bag. Loaders both for grouse and pheasant shooting normally receive a gratuity of about £10 per day from their guns in addition to whatever wage has been negotiated with the supplier.

On most shoots it is only the estate's keeper and not other helpers who should receive a tip. Where there is more than one keeper on an estate it is as well to consult with the host or shoot organiser. In any event the payment should always be made to the headkeeper who will then distribute the total largesse amongst his staff.

A stalker for both roe and red deer would normally receive a tip from his rifle for every day that they have spent together, regardless of whether or not a beast has been shot. The normal gratuity would be £10 per day but if an exceptional stag or buck has been killed then this amount may be considerably increased.

The person who is invited to a little rough-shooting by a friendly farmer could aptly show his gratitude by presenting a little of the standard rural bartering currency, a bottle of whisky. Such farmers are real gems so don't be mean – make it a good malt.

FANKLED POINTERS, preparing for a day over dogs. (*John Andrews*)

6 The Grouse

DOGGING

AUGUST - WHEN A shooter's fancy lightly turns to thoughts of grouse . . . 'Dear God, please let me get an invite to the first day over dogs!'

At last, the phone rings, invitation procured. Fervent preparations, dubbining of neglected boots (inspiring good thoughts for future care), gun degreased and cartridge bag filled. Interminable days in between made bearable by compensatory activity involving refresher retrieving course for unfit labrador and pseudo-shooting of passing starlings with dummy cartridges.

Day of the twelfth dawns: unprompted, dog bounds into car at the lifting of the tailgate.

At the stackyard meeting place excitement rises. The old Admiral, bearing the mien that once struck terror in the German fleet, twinkles his way across the yard. Antique but immaculate tackety boots reflect the sunshine; neatly pressed, if threadbare, tweeds putting us all to shame. Issuing orders of the day, he marshals us aboard the battered and less than immaculate Land–rover.

Boneshaken and suffering cramp we disgorge into the heady freedom of the open hill, thankfully filling our lungs with the sweet air.

The delightful Nancy arrives, aristocratic quartet of pointers and setters in hand. Even these sophisticated and elegant creatures succumb to the mood with impatient squeaks and pirouette around their mistress, weaving a tangled web of leads to be deftly unravelled by feminine fingers. Amid the throng, proletarian labradors wander, elongated pink tongues drip saliva with excitement and lack of fitness. We, in similar condition, struggle to make ready for the hill, stumbling over and cursing the electric spaniels as they bounce beneath our feet.

An old cock grouse cackles beyond the rise and spurs on our efforts. So does the Admiral. Precisely he regiments his guns behind the dogs. We head for high ground, giving dogs maximum scenting benefit from the light breeze. Yet unsupple boots chafe at the ankle, steep is the slope, rank heather stems ensnare the legs at every plod, wheezing, puffing and muttered curses fill the air.

Nancy leads on. The first dog down, unusual on a Scottish moor; Barry, her Irish setter, only one of the breed I know with a brain. Sheer joy to watch, reacting sharply to her every command, effortlessly and efficiently cruising across the heather, seeking game from the wind.

Nancy also delights the eye. Following a shapely rear in close-fitting tweed up the hill is a valuable spur for a shooter who is beginning to weary.

Straying thoughts are sharply brought back to focus on the business in hand. Barry is on point. Snaking forwards, nostrils locked on the line as the unseen birds scuttle through the heather stems, the setter freezes solid as they crouch to go no further. Tail extended and foreleg raised, a classic gold-bronze statue of elemental beauty. It seems sacrilege to disturb the scene.

Nancy insists. She waves we two guns forward to take the point. The heart is going like a steam hammer, palms sweating, knees beginning to wobble.

Soft female voice to the setter, 'Get on Barry.'

A brown blur as the covey rockets out, exploding in a burst of heather pollen, galvanising my old Dickson into its swing. . .

Yes, you do get hooked on it.

HOW FARES SCOTLAND'S PREMIER SPORTING BIRD?

The red grouse, *Lagopus lagopus scoticus*, has become an unofficial emblem of Scotland. The famous grouse has earned this status not just because of its connection with a brand of whisky but also because this supreme British gamebird is found nowhere else in the world. Although England may lay claim to some very fine grouse moors, principally in Yorkshire and Derbyshire, for the connoisseur, Scotland provides the quintessential backdrop for the sporting pursuit of what is widely acclaimed to be the finest and most testing gamebird in the world. Experience just one drive in a well-placed butt; strive to swing the gun far enough ahead of the brown bombshells, wind in their tails, scudding past, head high across the heather: you will then agree that they earn the accolade.

The grouse is a bird of the heather hill. It feeds almost exclusively on this plant, being particularly fond of the nourishing young shoots, while insects and berries, such as blaeberries, add a little variety. In hard winters of prolonged snow cover on the moors, great packs of hungry grouse may be seen descending to the low-ground stubble fields in search of lifesaving grain. Well-managed heather is the basic essential for production of a large shootable surplus of grouse.

Heather is a crop that requires skilful management, and a carefully tended moor may support a good grouse shoot as well as a moderate stock of sheep. In some areas there has been a temptation in the past to overstock with sheep, leading to overgrazing and the subsequent destruction of large areas of heather. Overgrazed heather rapidly deteriorates into rough grass, which is useless for both grouse and sheep.

Poor husbandry, a subsequent increase in predators, infestations of the grouse tick, over-grazing and universal bad management of the heather crop has meant that many moors suffered a decline since the big bag heydays of the 1930s. Now, however, the situation is beginning to improve, largely due to the growing demand for and value of grouse

shooting which is encouraging effective management and remedial action.

While grouse shooting is on the increase, hill sheep farming is becoming less profitable, and there are many landowners today who bitterly regret selling out large tracts of hilly ground to forestry interests. This acreage now under trees could have been producing a handsome annual return from sporting use. The prosperity of the local community also suffers where tree replaces grouse. Hill and moor smothered by sterile regiments of spruce attract few visitors, sporting or otherwise.

LOOKING AFTER GROUSE

Optimum conditions for grouse production depend on providing the bird with four basic controllable elements: food, shelter, protection from predators and freedom from disturbance at breeding time. Weather, the final uncontrollable ingredient, is crucially important when birds are nesting and in the first few weeks of the chicks' life. A dry warm spring is an essential factor in producing large, well-grown coveys in August.

What weather each area receives at vital times of year is in the lap of the gods. The moor keeper may be thoroughly conscientious and hard-working. He may manage his heather correctly by burning, regenerating and preventing overgrazing, he may spend countless long hours controlling predators and have immaculate lines of butts, but a cloudburst in June could decimate his season's stock of young birds. The galling thing is that it may be just his side of the glen that is affected,

while the neighbouring estate on the other side may stay in sunshine and have a super season.

Good grouse moors do not occur naturally. Much time, money and effort is required to put good coveys over the butts. But lacking divine ability, the moor manager must confine himself to the controllable factors. Wet and boggy ground does not produce good heather and must be drained if maximum production is to be achieved. The moor must contain a diverse patchwork of old long-stemmed heather to provide cover for nesting and shelter, interspersed with feeding areas of succulent young shoots. This patchwork is achieved quite simply over the years by judicious muirburn during March and early April, when smoke from the keepers' fires is a familiar sight in grouse country. Burning off old dry heather which has no food value soon produces a regenerating crop of new shoots, highly nutritious and attractive to grouse.

Foxes, crows and stoats are the main moorland predators and many hours of the keeper's time must be spent in controlling their numbers.

On moors where there is little available natural grit, an essential for the bird's digestive process, it is necessary to distribute supplies of commercially produced grit.

Grouse keepers are sometimes subject to the horrors of an influx of heather beetle which may deplete the food supply dramatically. This scourge of the moors flourishes in mild winters and is to *Calluna vulgaris* what the greenfly is to roses. Like the grouse its principal diet is heather, but unlike the grouse the appetite of the beetle soon turns large acreages of the plant into brown blocks of useless bare twigs. It is economically impossible to control this pest artificially but nature, given a chance, does have a remedy. There is a parasitic wasp which normally takes advantage of such a plentitude of its favourite food. When the beetle multiplies so does its predator, and usually the plague is reduced to a level which prevents further devastation of the heather. One of the snags is that heather burning will destroy the parasitic wasp and therefore areas infested by the beetle should be spared the torch.

Another little 'nasty' that directly attacks the grouse, causing dramatic crashes in the population when heavy infections occur, is the trichostrongyle worm. Infected birds simply waste away and breeding success is obviously very limited. If birds are able to be caught there is a treatment which will cure this worm, but although some infested estates have made an attempt at this by netting roosting grouse at night and dosing them, treatment on a large scale is obviously impractical.

Other duties of the moorland keeper include maintenance of butts and hill roads. Preserving traditional butts is a skilled business as 'heather bricks' need to be cut by hand and fitted into the walls of the butt. The process is almost like dry stone dyking with peat instead of stone.

Most estates have suitable machinery to assist in keeping hill tracks in good order, but this may still use up a large slice of the keeper's time. Grouse require a peaceful, undisturbed period in the spring if they are to hatch and rear their chicks successfully, but springtime may also signal an influx of hill-walkers to the moor, many of whom will simply not appreciate or care about the damage they may do if they are permitted to wander unchecked through nesting areas. The keeper must practice the highest forms of diplomacy at times if he is to prevent excessive disturbance.

All this effort must be expended on the wild birds because grouse, unlike pheasants, do not readily lend themselves to artificial rearing practices. It is simply not practical or financially feasible to augment grouse numbers by reared birds.

SHOOTING METHODS

Grouse are shot in three different ways, driving, over dogs, and walking up.

On moors with large grouse densities, driving is the traditionally accepted method, producing a class of shooting that is unmatched for challenge and excitement.

Shooting over dogs is generally employed on moors with sparser populations. Pointers and setters are the time-honoured breeds for this work, evoking a classical atmosphere of yester-year, although the beautiful Irish setter and various continental hunt, point and retrieve breeds like the Weimaraner, Vizsla and German short-haired pointer are also used. To anyone with a hunter's soul there is no more stirring sight than an aristocratic pair of English pointers or setters quartering the moor, freezing on point as they indicate the hidden presence of a covey. The dog-handler will invite two of the shooting team to come forward, one on each side of the pointing dog, which will then be ordered to flush the covey, providing a variety of testing shots as the birds rise. Traditionally referred to as 'dogging', this is an efficient means of locating birds on vast expanses of ground and usually involves considerable exertion for the guns, with several miles of rough moorland being covered in the course of the day.

Walking-up is a common method on less prestigious moors where a line of guns proceeds across the ground, often with the assistance of some spaniels which find and flush game in front of the line. The bags achieved in this way and by dogging are normally much less than on driven shoots, and a reasonable degree of physical fitness is required by participants.

A DRIVEN DAY

A day's grouse driving will usually commence with the arrival of transport at the lodge or hotel where the shooting party is accommodated. Most good moors have a rough hill road system which permits easy access by all-terrain vehicles to within reasonable walking distance or even right up to the butts. Lines of butts are placed at strategic locations around the moor, often running up and down the face of a hill on flight lines that have been noted over the years. The purpose of the butt is to conceal most of the shooter as grouse are wary birds, easily diverted by the sight of the human figure. Traditional butts are made from stone or turf, designed to blend with the landscape although more easily constructed but obtrusive wooden ones are employed on some estates. The host or head keeper will assign guns to specified butts by a process of drawing numbers. On subsequent drives guns will move up two places. It is a strict safety rule that no shot must be taken as birds cross through the line of butts unless they are directly overhead or well above the height of neighbouring guns. Some butts are furnished with idiot-proof poles on each side to prevent the over-enthusiastic and careless gun from peppering his neighbour in the heat of the moment.

On prestigious moors where there are heavy stocks of grouse double guns are often used, requiring the services of a loader. Practice is needed to master the technique of efficiently changing guns and when this is perfected a high rate of fire is possible.

Grouse drives take in very large tracts of land and last a good deal longer than pheasant drives. Often there are lengthy waits until the arrival of the first bird, which could take the unwary gun by surprise.

As a good deal of grouse shooting takes place in August and September, students commonly make up the bulk of the beating team. As the drive starts they may be seen on a distant skyline waving their white flags. Some of them are utilised as 'flankers' who are placed well out ahead and to the side of the line of butts. It is their job to deflect birds which are breaking out to the side by suddenly springing up out of the heather and vigorously flapping their flags in an attempt to turn the birds. Ribald cries when they are unsuccessful occasionally drift across the moor.

Total concentration to the front is essential for the guns as grouse often seem to appear from nowhere and are long gone before the gunstock is into the shoulder. Birds may come to the butts singly, in small groups or coveys up to 20 in number or, later in the season, sometimes in huge packs of 100 or so at a time. When the birds are coming straight at the butt it is necessary to shoot when they appear to be out of range. By the time the brain registers the decision to fire they will have travelled a long way and be well within

R ED GROUSE cock.
(*Roger Tidman*)

range. Unless a decision is made to shoot early the gun will find himself desperately stumbling to turn round in the butt and fire at a covey departing with supersonic speed.

The shooting party will have been advised by the host or keeper that a horn or whistle will be blown as a signal that no more shots may be taken in front as the beating line approaches within the danger zone. Guns will then turn round and take shots only at birds that have passed through the line of butts.

Guns are expected roughly to mark and keep a mental tally of where the shot birds fall. The pickers-up have been waiting well behind the line of butts with their retrievers, collecting any bird that was hit but carried on to fall far behind. As the keeper blows the final call to signify the end of the drive, the pickers-up confer with the guns and send their dogs to scour the heather for the fallen. Then its back to the Land-rovers and off to the next drive.

LOCATIONS AND COSTS

Even in Scotland, which is after all the real home of red grouse shooting, such is the popularity of the sport that the best is always much sought after. The demand seems to increase every year despite the fact that driven grouse shooting in particular is, by its very nature, extremely expensive. Visitors wishing to arrange to shoot grouse in Scotland should commence initial enquiries at least nine months prior to the proposed visit, and it is likely that a greater choice would be available if bookings were made a year in advance.

At 1990 prices the average rate for driven

grouse shooting was £90 per brace, walked up grouse were £40 per brace, and walked up over dogs the rate was £40 plus the cost of the dogs. All these prices were subject to VAT at the rate of 15 per cent. To work out the individual cost per gun for driven grouse the price per brace should be multiplied by the agreed prospective bag and then divided by the number of guns taking part. For example, for a 70 brace day:

£90 brace × 70 bag = £6300 divided among 8 guns = £788 plus VAT per gun.

The various undernoted estates and agencies will ensure that their clients receive quality sport at an appropriate price.

Strathspey Estates

Sport let in conjunction with Kinveachy Lodge in glorious Strathspey. Although the estate normally lets one week's walked up grouse shooting, most of the birds are shot driven to a party of eight or more guns on the basis of there being five day's shooting and one day's salmon fishing on the rest day during the course of any week. Tenants normally arrive on the Sunday afternoon or evening and leave the following Sunday morning. The sporting rent for a week's grouse shooting would depend on the expected bag, but where 400–650 brace are offered over the five days, this is likely to be between £28,000 and £45,000 plus VAT for the party.

Contact: The Factor, Strathspey Estate Office, Grantown-on-Spey, Moray, PH26 3HQ. Tel: 0479 2529. Fax: 0479 3452.

Scone Estates

From 12 August to early October, Scone Estates offer driven grouse shooting in Perthshire for parties of seven to nine guns, most coming for a four-day week. Bags in excess of 100 brace may be achieved early in the season, while 50 brace may be a nearer expectation later in the season when the birds begin to pack. A sample rent for a day's driven grouse, expecting about 80 brace for eight guns for the day, would be in the region of £6,000 plus VAT.

Contact: The Factor, Estates Office, Scone Palace, Perth, PH2 6BD. Tel: 0738 52308. Fax: 0738 52588.

Sport in Scotland Ltd

Driven: The company offers driven grouse shooting on four estates in Inverness-shire and four estates in Perthshire. Three, four and five-day periods are generally available for parties of eight or nine using single guns. There is one estate in Perthshire which may require double guns when loaders will be provided at an additional rate of £40 per person per day. Sample price: £4,200 plus VAT for nine guns shooting 40 to 60 brace. Walked-up: Three moors in Perthshire and one in Inverness-shire. Sample price: £1,265 including VAT for five or six guns shooting about 20 brace. Over pointers: It is possible to arrange the use of pointers on several moors and this would be at a price of £115 per day including VAT for a man and a pointer.

The company will arrange suitable accommodation if required.

Contact: Sport in Scotland Ltd, 22, Market Brae, Inverness, IV2 3AB. Tel: 0463 222757/232104. Telex: 75446.

Macsport Ltd

This company has extensive grouse shooting throughout the north–east from the finest driven moors to modest walked up days. Macsport also operate fieldsport and photographic courses.

This sample of a typical grouse weekend run by Macsport consists of two days' driven shooting at Edinglassie, Huntly, Aberdeenshire, which would be expected to produce 100 brace in total. Accommodation is provided in Avochie House at Huntly and all meals, drinks and transportation are provided. Cartridges will be provided at extra cost on a sale or return basis. The cost of the shooting for a party of eight guns including three nights accommodation at Avochie House is £6,880 plus VAT. Extra non-shooting guests may accompany the party at £330 per head plus VAT.

Contact: Macsport Ltd, Ballater Road, Aboyne, Aberdeenshire, AB3 5HT. Tel: 03398 86896. Fax: 03398 86291.

Invery House, Aberdeenshire

Grouse shooting is available in the Deeside area to hotel guests at around the following prices: driven – £85–£95 plus VAT per brace, walked up – £40–£45 plus VAT per brace, over dogs – £40–£45 plus VAT per brace.

Contact: Stewart Spence, Invery House, Banchory, Royal Deeside, Kincardineshire,

AB3 3NJ. Tel: 03302 4782. Telex: 73737. Fax: 03302 4712.

Alvie Estate

Driven and walked up grouse shooting offered on the estate. Prices are available on application. Lodge and self-catering accommodation available.

Contact: Nick Lewtas, Alvie Estate Office, Kincraig, Kingussie, Inverness-shire, PH21 1NE. Tel: 05404 255/249. Fax: 05404 380.

Game International

Driven and walked up grouse shooting available in Aberdeenshire. All types of accommodation arranged. Prices at normal rates.

Contact: Game International Ltd, The Firs, Mount Blairy, Banff, Aberdeenshire, AB4 3XN. Tel: 0888 68618. Fax: 0888 63950.

Scaliscro, Isle of Lewis

Grouse over pointers on estates in the west of Lewis, including snipe shooting. September to November. Expected bag is from five to eight brace mixed. Gamekeeper, ghillie, pointers and argocat supplied. Cost: £300 plus VAT. 'MacNabs' also arranged (full details in red deer section).

Contact: Estates Office, Scaliscro, Uig, Isle of Lewis, PA86 9EL. Tel: 085175 325. Fax: 085175 393.

Major Neil Ramsay

Traditional grouse over pointers on very extensive estates in Aberdeenshire, Banffshire and Caithness for groups of two or three guns. Expectation 15 brace per group/day. Programmes of two to four day's shooting. Charges from £620 to £690 plus VAT per group/day, including keeper, dog handlers and transport. Accommodation extra.

Driven grouse in Angus and Inverness-shire. Parties of eight or nine guns. Expectation 50 to 70 brace per day. Programmes of two to three days. Charges around £615 plus VAT per gun/day. Accommodation extra.

Contact: Major Neil Ramsay, Tay Terrace, Dunkeld. Perthshire, PH8 0AQ. Tel: 03502 8991. Fax: 03502 8800.

Tweed Valley Hotel, Peeblesshire

Driven or walked up grouse available in Peeblesshire in the Borders for parties of six to eight guns with bags ranging from 10 to 50 brace days. Also mixed days of blackcock and grouse. Mostly modest bags at modest prices. Accommodation in the hotel which has clayshooting practice facilities in the grounds.

Contact: Charles Miller, Tweed Valley Hotel, Walkerburn, Peeblesshire, 6SAA EH43. Tel: 089687 636. Fax: 089687 639.

John Andrews Sporting

Traditional grouse over pointers and setters or walked up on moors from East Lothian to Caithness. Bags from two and a half brace to ten brace per gun. Prices from £100 to £150 per gun/day. One- to six-day programmes available. Limited driven days.

Contact: John Andrews, Muirside House, Bellies Brae, Kirriemuir, Angus, DD8 4EB. Tel: 0575 74350.

East Haugh House Hotel, Perthshire

Walked up grouse over pointers is available on two moors in Perthshire for hotel guests. The proprietors also organise guided shooting trips to the Western Isles involving very interesting mixed sport which includes walked up grouse. Prices are available on application.

Contact: Neil McGown, East Haugh House, By Pitlochry, Perthshire, PH16 5JS. Tel: 0796 3121.

Cultoquhey House Hotel, Perthshire

Driven, walked up and over dogs grouse shooting is available on Perthshire moors for guests of the hotel. Individuals and parties of up to 12 guns are catered for.

Contact: David Cooke, Cultoquhey House Hotel, By Crieff, Perthshire, PH7 3NE. Tel: 0764 3253.

R F Watson, Scottish Sporting Agent

A varied range of grouse shooting from full driven days to modest walking days is available on moors from the Borders to Caithness. Sample prices: walked up – £150 per gun per day; over pointers in Caithness, averaging two and a half brace per gun – £100 per gun per day.

Contact: R F Watson, Scottish Sporting Agent, Jubilee Cottage, Fowlis Wester, Perthshire, PH7 3NI. Tel: 0764 83468. Fax: 0764 83475.

7 The Pheasant

THE MELANISTIC

AS THE LAZY pink fingers of dawn crawled across the Perthshire hills the old cock fluffed out his feathers and threw his arrogant call out across the wood in greeting.

The gnarled Scots Pine in which he had spent many nights of this the third winter of his long life gradually took on its sage green colour of day, its russet bark emerging into life as it absorbed the cool early light creeping through the wood. The pheasant was hungry; he had missed his late afternoon feed on the stubble adjoining his roosting wood.

The previous day, Robert Cairney, the tenant who farmed this part of Edradarnoch estate, had decided to take advantage of the recent spell of dry weather to commence ploughing the field adjoining Lurgan wood. It would stand another crop of barley and he was anxious to sow it out before winter really started to bite. He had spied the black cock pheasant in mid afternoon as it nervously fussed in and out of the base of the thick beech hedge which separated the field from the wood. He knew his presence with throbbing tractor and clanking plough was keeping the bird from its evening's picking on the stubble which he was rapidly turning into rich virgin ridges of earth. He almost regarded the bird as an old friend. He had first noticed it two years

ago – being black it stood out dramatically from the other more commonly coloured pheasants. Robert had grown to admire the bird. It was always the first to leg it for cover when he appeared in view, long before the other birds had even raised their heads in alarm. He smiled as he saw it hesitating on the edge of the field.

'Cunning old bastard,' he muttered. 'You're far too damn crafty to ever get shot, you'll be on your bike before the beaters even get into the wood.'

Shooting was very much on his mind as he ploughed. Every year the laird invited him to a day at driven pheasants. Tomorrow was the day and he was always a bit nervous beforehand. It was not just that he would be embarrassed if he did not shoot well, but being a formal shoot he had to watch that he observed all the niceties of shooting etiquette and safety. He hurried to finish the field before dusk. He could hardly afford to take a day off on the morrow but he could never turn down such an invitation. The grey curtain of dusk was fast drawing as he ploughed the last end-rig.

With a final throaty crow at the dawn the melanistic cock clattered down from the pine. His normal inclination was to forage out over the stubble and hedgerows in order to fill his crop for the day. He was a wild bird, hatched far out on the hill in a rushy hollow on the

edge of the moor. He was used to seeking out his own food and he scorned the easy life led by the many hundreds of reared birds on the estate. They were heavier, fatter birds than he and most did not stray far from the coverts where they could easily fill their crops on the wheat provided daily by the keeper. He now avoided this fast food convenience. To him it meant danger.

As a first year bird, he was often lured by the easy pickings to be had at the woodland feeds. Whilst stuffing his crop at a wheat hopper, a sudden intrusion of noise caused him to join his reared cousins in taking to their heels, running in fright from the presence of men at the end of the wood. His natural inclination was to hide himself and this he did, tucking himself completely out of sight beneath a pile of spruce brashings. The noise approached, a heavy panting and sniffing sounded close by and suddenly his pile of branches heaved upwards as he felt the hot breath of a bustling spaniel, blood up and eager to seize his hidden body.

'Millie, you bastard!' roared the springer's owner as it took off in delinquent pursuit of the swiftly exiting pheasant. The bitch ignored the beater's desperate cry of 'Come in here you little shit!' as with a final eager bound it seized the pheasants's rump. True to his wild nature, the pheasant struck out rapidly with his junior spurs, catching the corner of Millie's eye. The pain forced her to relax her grip. Amidst a flying flourish of black-bronze feathers the cock battered its way up through the canopy of branches, raining down a stream of brittle spruce needles on the head of the thwarted spaniel left gagging and chewing at a mouthful of tail feathers, shrinking in dread from the purposeful and menacing approach of its irate master.

The cock knew where he wanted to be – back at the lonely fringes of the moor. Ignoring the many shots out in front, he set himself for home. Without a tail his flight was clumsy as he approached the line of guns. The laird smiled as the black bird headed over the right hand gun. It was his youngest son and the pheasant, now climbing fast, would provide a testing shot. His shout of 'Over, Jamie!' was unnecessary. The youngster was already tracking the bird with upraised muzzles and as it approached almost overhead he went back on his heel in classic style, starting to swing his gun from behind, following through, out ahead of the beak. The fractional hesitation, as he realised there was something different about this one, jarred his swing. Close behind his denuded rear the pheasant felt the hot rush of pellets.

For the rest of that winter he kept the company of grouse and blackcock, feeding frugally on grass seeds and insects with an occasional nervous visit to the easier pickings of hill farm oat stubbles and turnip fields rich in weed seeds. He managed to withstand an occasional skirmish with Old Harry Martin, the hill farm tenant, who was partial to roast pheasant and not above discharging his ancient hammer gun in the direction of a bird when 'the gamie' was well out of the way.

The following winter saw the cock move his quarters to the lower ground where, when hungry, he succumbed to an occasional hasty trip to the coverts and the keeper's winter feeds. He would tolerate but rapidly distance himself from occasional human company in the form of the tractor driver or shepherd, but would keep on running when he sighted Old Harry. On his sporadic visits to the woods he would instantly take to his heels and head far out on the moor whenever he sensed approaching groups of men and dogs.

This morning the strong cold east wind and snow flurries fuelled his hunger, lending him a careless arrogance. A quick trip to the feed hopper with its compelling free issue of tasty wheat would quickly fill his empty crop. Just down the hill from his roost in the Lurgan wood was one of the main coverts on the estate, Cluny Brae. This was a large warm mixed wood which ran due east and west across the lower slopes of the hill. Dave Cameron, the keeper, had a large release pen there where he had carefully tended a thousand pheasant poults since July. There was always plenty of feed to be had there. As the cock scurried downhill towards Cluny Brae keeping in the shelter of the old stone dyke, Robert Cairney was forking the last few graipfuls of silage into his cattle court. Grabbing gun and cartridge bag he quickly drove the short distance to the Big House where the other invited guns were assembling.

He was relieved when his host made a point of greeting him like a brother and guided him round the assembled company introducing him to the other guests. He felt a little out of place as many of his fellow guns were wealthy land-owners or prominent businessmen and he inwardly squirmed a little, desperately seeking for the correct form of address for the distinguished noble lord he had noticed in the company. His dilemma was soon resolved as the aristocratic hand was extended.

'Pleased to meet you, Robert. I'm Archie.'

Robert relaxed as he chatted with the peer about Beef Short-horns, a mutual interest. He hoped he could be as relaxed about his shooting. He knew most of the other guns were ace shots and most desperately he wanted to perform well. The laird came round proferring to each gun an elegant pigskin wallet containing small numbered ivory tags. Each in turn drew a tag from the wallet, thus establishing which of the eight numbered pegs they would stand at for the first drive.

'Usual form, gentlemen,' projected the laird, switching into his commander mode. 'The pins number from left to right and you move up two for each drive. Four drives in the morning and three after lunch. No shooting after David blows his horn at the end of each drive. No ground game to be shot. Take as many pigeons, crows and jays as you can but don't shoot low birds or my white pheasants. Please remember the beaters in front and pickers-up behind and don't be putting any shots near them. Slight change of plan this morning. This damned gale from the east will make it difficult to push the birds out of Cluny Brae in the usual way. Today the beat will take it in the opposite direction and we'll stand at the west end. It's a little awkward because of the den but standing down there we should get some bloody sporting shots.'

As the Land-rovers churned over barley stubble towards the west end of Cluny Brae wood Robert cursed. He realised that having drawn number one he would be at the uphill end of Cluny Den, the deep gully through which the Cluny burn rushed on its way to join the river Tay. This was the deepest part of the den, which meant that any birds coming over him would be high and ultra-testing. Very fast shooting would be required as they would be on him before he could see them. He wished he could have had an easy peg to start with. His confidence needed a boost.

The guns disgorged from the Land-rovers, footering with guns and cartridge bags, speaking in lowered tones, not wishing to disturb the birds in covert.

'Quiet, Jamie, for God's sake,' hissed the laird as the vehicle's door was carelessly slammed by his daydreaming son.

Greedily pecking at the wheat hopper, way up in the middle of Cluny Brae, the old melanistic cock caught the sound. He was off – long spurred legs covered the ground at high speed. Several times he had done this before. His established escape route was up a bramble-covered ditch at the end of the wood where the guns normally stood. Even at times when numbers seven and eight guns were already in position on each side of the ditch he could still escape unseen as he scuttled away beneath the bramble fronds.

The guns usually spoke in whispers. This time the human sound was louder. Ribald comments, whistles and shouted instructions caused him to hasten on up the ditch. He had made a big mistake.

Millie was not quite as fast as she had been three years ago but the spaniel had never been cured of pegging live pheasants. Busting the brambles apart as she quested the ditch bottom her grabbing jaws just missed the cock as he almost collided with her. Flushing like an Exocet right off her nose he launched himself vertically on the gale, his flight plan set for the Lurgan wood and safety. The beaters cheered as he headed downwind following the line of the wood straight towards the lefthand guns. David, the keeper, paused to watch as the bird lifted high with the east wind under his tail. 'There's a cracker, Tam!' he called to Millie's owner. 'Good wee girl,' muttered Tam benevolently.

The first bird over the angst-suffering Robert Cairney was a screamingly high pigeon. Pigeons were Robert's speciality as he often shot them of an evening coming into roost. He killed it in exquisite style. 'Thank God', he breathed, blissfully aware that the laird, next peg down, was watching him. As he reloaded, the laird's shout indicated two hens curling across the wind in tandem. 'Yours, Robert!'

Confidence and well-being swung his consecutive shots exactly where needed. Both hens collapsed to splash down within feet of each other, straight into Cluny burn giving the picker-up a few anxious moments until her labrador Teal cleverly emerged with both at the same time. In his triumphal moment Robert felt magnanimous. 'Good on you, Sally. Two at a time!'

The distant roar from the beaters caused gun, laird and picker-up to gaze skywards. Out in front the highest pheasant the Laird had ever seen soared on set wings, gliding way above the den towards the left hand gun.

'And again, Robert!' bellowed the laird, wishing to God that the bird had come to him, and resignedly waiting for it to crumple. Robert was glowing with confidence. This was the bird that would really make his name. As his eager barrels swung up behind the cock its plumage caught a blink of sharp winter sun. It flashed – not chestnut but black. Perhaps it wasn't him? The instant's hesitation cost him his moment. His shot pattern that had found nothing but empty air fell harmlessly on his new-ploughed stubble five hundred yards away.

It was more than a year later before he saw the black cock pheasant again. It was Hogmanay and Old Harry had come calling knowing that Robert usually had a goodly supply of malt on hand.

'Here you go, Bob.' With an impish wink, Harry handed over a Tesco's plastic bag. 'Thought you might like a tasty wee bird for yer New Year's dinner. Got the bugger from the pick-up window. Nailed him scoffing ma feed from the sheep's trough away o'er the moor.'

Drawing the body from the plastic bag, Robert instantly understood Harry's uncharacteristic generosity. The bird was an ancient melanistic cock, black breast sharp as a razor blade and with spurs nearly two inches long.

ORIGIN AND DEVELOPMENT OF THE PHEASANT AS A SPORTING BIRD

These days there are probably more cartridges detonated in the direction of *Phasianus colchicus*, the common game pheasant, than at any other game species in Scotland. Yet this ideal sporting bird is but a stranger to our shores, not an indigenous species. Originally the bird was a native of the vast marshlands of Asia, a type of habitat of which it is still inordinately fond. It does not really belong amidst the lofty oaks and beeches of the traditional British game coverts.

It appears that the sportsmen of today owe the presence of this bird to the ease with which the English nation habitually allowed itself to be overrun with invaders. It was the conquering Romans who, with their penchant for the good things in life, brought with them a particularly tasty form of poultry in the form of the domesticated pheasant. Rather than pursuing fresh meat they obviously preferred to have these tasty morsels on hand, thus saving their energies for futile forays into Scotland. The wild men of mist and mountains may have repelled the Romans but the pheasant eventually made it across the border, providing today an alternative sporting target for Scottish aggression.

Rearing of game birds for sport began in England around the end of the eighteenth century. This took place in a limited way as the sporting arms in use at the time were muzzle-loading percussion weapons and the very cumbersome and awkward nature of

reloading precluded any sustained rate of fire. Towards the end of the nineteenth century, having become the proud possessors of sporting guns which could now be loaded with convenient cartridges, the sportsmen of the day wanted to make full use of this increased fire power. Despite the fact that all early breech–loading guns were hammer guns without ejectors, which required more dexterity and manipulation than the ubiquitous hammerless guns in use today, impressive rates of fire were achieved by these sportsmen. But on wintry mornings when a sudden flush of birds crowded the sky, those within range of the shooter so armed were often in mortal danger: accidental discharges were commonplace as frozen fingers fumbled with the awkward hammers. For safety reasons alone we must be thankful that the gunmakers, rising to the occasion, were not long in producing the safer and more efficient hammerless shotgun. Fuelled by the vogue for invention and innovation which marked the tenor of the times, this improvement in sporting arms came about largely as a direct response to the needs of driven game shooting and fashionable big bags.

Prior to the era of the 'big shots' the native partridge was the main sporting bird on low-ground estates, and this wild-bred, home-grown product did not readily lend itself to mass production methods. The English lords of the manor had found that the pheasant provided the ideal bird for mass rearing techniques. It also adapted readily to the woodlands and policies surrounding their stately homes where it could be held in covert

and guaranteed to provide reliable sport and impressive numbers when and where required.

Later, during the heyday of the fashionable Victorian shooting parties with their infamous battues, aristocrats with extensive estates vied with each other to provide the highest number of slain at what amounted to little more than organised mass slaughter. The quality of birds presented was of little account so long as at the day's end there were large piles of dead bodies to be tallied and compared with that of their neighbours.

Such mayhem was made possible by the availability of low-cost labour which was necessary to support the highly labour-intensive methods of game rearing and preservation of these times. The big estates supported small armies of sturdy yeomen who were well used to the long hours and hard graft demanded by the keepering profession. Happily the big estates could afford to employ often as many as 20 or 30 keepers who worked round the clock to ensure that their master's acreage was jammed full with as many pheasants as it could provide ground space for.

The rearing method then employed was to have this army of keepers (and often their families) scour the woods and hedgerows for pheasants nesting in the wild. Once the nests were located, regular visits were made to collect the eggs which, provided at least one egg had been left in the nest, the hen bird would obligingly keep supplying. Often as many as 30 eggs per nest were collected in this way. Artificial eggs were sometimes employed to fool the hen into thinking that she had not been robbed and to encourage her to continue production.

The general practice used today of catching up birds and confining them in pens for egg production was not in general use at the time as, apart from other considerations, wire netting was not generally available and therefore penning pheasants in any quantity posed considerable practical problems. The relative scarcity of foxes, stoats, weasels, grey squirrels, crows, jays, magpies and all species of predatory birds created an environment in which wild game-birds could reproduce with impunity. Wildlife legislation of the time permitted the wholesale destruction of any creature which might have the temerity even to glance at a pheasant egg or poult. Anything with a hooked beak was an enemy of the game preserver and many devious and barbarous means were employed in an attempt to bring about their total annihilation. In some cases their efforts were completely successful and such short-sighted policies led to species like the red kite, goshawk and osprey being reduced to a state of extinction in the British Isles.

Farming practices at this time greatly favoured the survival and well-being of all forms of game and many other wildlife species. The survival of some of these species is hanging in the balance today due to incompatible modern agricultural practices. In the late Victorian era, the many thick hedgerows which contained the small fields of the time provided good nesting cover and winter shelter, and stubble fields remained intact until the spring time, providing attractive winter feeding. The widespread practice of utilising turnips as main winter feed ensured that there was a patchwork throughout the countryside of attractive cover providing incidental feeding. At hatching time young pheasant and partridge chicks flourished on the huge variety of insect life which was readily available to them in the organically fertilised and naturally grown cereal fields. The chemically treated sterile prairies of today's barley factories are efficiently productive but yield only a meagre harvest of game.

By creating an environment which was very much in favour of wild bird production, the supply of reared game on late nineteenth-century estates was substantially supplemented by a flourishing stock of naturally produced birds.

As automatic electronic incubators were unknown at the time, the only means available for artificially rearing vast numbers of pheasants was by the use of the 'broody hen' system. This method required a plentiful supply of obliging hens or bantams which had reached the stage of advanced maternity which compelled them to sit optimistically on any available egg. Today such devotion to family life has largely been bred out of our poultry: the broody hen is a rare beast, ephemeral as the Holy Grail – as many a frustrated home rearer of pheasants can testify. The old-time keeper had no such worries as every country dweller had plenty of natural living hens scratching about the doors. Such birds were liable to go broody at the drop of a hat, providing a readily available and reliable source of incubation.

The other basic requirement for this system was an adequate supply of coops. These were little wooden houses with slatted fronts which accommodated the broody and her surrogate family. These coops were arranged in serried ranks on the chosen rearing field of short mown grass. A shift system of unfortunate underkeepers was deployed to live out the summer in a primitive caravan based on the rearing field. It was essential to maintain a human presence both night and day, not only to feed and water the hens but also to repel foxes and other miscreants who would swiftly take advantage of an unprotected ready meal. When the chicks hatched, the foster mother hen was retained in the coop and her brood allowed access to the outside world by coming and going through the spars. Being the first living creature which they encountered on hatching the chicks became malimprinted by the hen and came to regard her as their natural mother. The keeper's vigil then intensified. Lots of tasty wee morsels running about an open field was like a free cafeteria to winged and four-legged predators. Many a hawk and falcon met its end on the rearing field and foxes that insisted on dining regularly on young pheasant were shown no mercy even in the vulpine-worshipping hunting counties.

Feeding this multitude was a major exercise and a wide variety of recipes was concocted, most originating from copious boilers into which large numbers of rabbit carcasses were consigned. Ant eggs were thought to be highly efficacious for the well-being of young pheasants and many a weary keeper spent many a weary hour attempting to collect enough to feed his charges.

Having reached about six weeks of age the total household of each coop-unit was laboriously transferred to the appropriate covert. The continued presence of their foster parent encouraged the poults to regard that neck of the woods as home base. As they grew the keepers ensured that they were hand fed daily, summoning them with a call that the poults soon learned to recognise and respond to. The birds continued to be cherished and nurtured until they suffered the rude awakening of an October dawn and the first shoot of the season.

The Scottish lairds were not overlong in aping the squires of the English counties in taking up pheasant production in this way. Most of the Lowlands provided suitable climate and habitat and even in the more northerly Highlands, particularly in the east, there were many fertile straths where the pheasant could flourish. Perhaps partly due to the traditionally parsimonious nature of Scottish landowners, which dissuaded them from indulging in overstocking their pheasant coverts, and partly due to the more generally hilly nature of the terrain, the sport in Scotland developed on a higher plane. With fewer birds and steeper ground, the quality of pheasants shown to the guns became para-mount. Excessive bags declined in importance as Scottish hosts took more pride in providing testing shots for their guests. In any event Scottish guns, used to shooting driven grouse, found little challenge in executing masses of bumbling, head-high, semi-tame pheasants. Thus Scotland became the Mecca for the connoisseur of quality sport.

Pheasant shooting in Scotland has changed dramatically over the last 25 years. No estate owner then, and very few now, set out to develop pheasant shooting primarily as a commercial proposition. Originally landowners managed their shooting solely for their own and their guests' pleasure. In recent years, vastly increased costs of staff, equipment, feed and the general expenses of running a large estate meant that many owners could no longer afford to utilise the sporting potential of their ground solely as a recreational pursuit for themselves, and they began to let the occasional day as a means of defraying costs. This situation coincided with an increase in demand for driven game shooting, much of which arose from increasing numbers of overseas visitors wishing to come to Scotland to shoot. At the same time the domestic demand for leasing shooting, both by the day and season, began to grow and the last few years have seen a great upsurge in the use of pheasant shooting as an attractive activity for corporate entertainment purposes.

Recently national agricultural policy has veered away from maximising production towards reducing output through such devices as 'set aside' schemes and finding alternative uses for land. As agricultural incomes fell, landowners and farmers began to develop the recreational and leisure potential of their land. All forms of shooting may produce worthwhile revenue and with the improvements in modern rearing techniques, pheasant shooting became more attractive as a commercial concern. It would not be possible for an estate to be financially viable if it were to rely solely on the revenue generated by game shooting, but the sport does produce a useful additional income and also helps to maintain the attractive non-commercial woodlands, hedgerows, wetlands and other agriculturally non-productive environments. These habitats form the basis of Scotland's rural landscape and incidentally assist in supporting many other forms of wildlife.

Thus game shooting is becoming more available to a wider section of the public, land-owners are receiving valuable income, rural landscapes are restored and improved, wildlife habitats are preserved and visitors to Scotland have an increasing number of shooting venues available and a wider choice of sport. A major advantage of this development is that the growing sphere of shooting tourism generates increasing and much needed economic benefits in many rural areas.

Obviously, pheasants do not appear by magic. Although there are some shoots which produce reasonable sport by relying solely on wild birds, ground which is to sustain any number of driven days has to depend on released birds to establish the necessary stock. Rearing pheasants is an expensive business. On most shoots the true cost of putting a reared pheasant over the guns may well be as high as £20 per bird. Ironically, in recent seasons, once the bird is shot its wholesale market value varies between 50p and £1. Economies of scale may reduce the production cost figure to below £15 per bird, but there is no great profit margin to the landowner when the going rate for commercial shooting in recent years is priced out at around £15 per bird. Commercial pheasant shooting is sold mainly as individual days, arranged for a party of normally around eight guns. The standard bag offered is approximately 200 birds which works out at an individual cost per gun of £375, exclusive of VAT. Larger or smaller bags may be purchased on a pro rata basis.

With the increasing demand for shooting, particularly from European and American visitors, a relatively new profession has developed in Scotland, the sporting agent. The agent will act as middle man between the landowner and prospective customer. In addition to arranging shooting to suit the demands of clients, in most cases he will undertake total arrangements for visiting parties or individuals. Some offer package deals which take care of travel arrangements, gun permits, accommodation and every other need of the visiting sportsman. Some estates prefer to deal directly with clients and there are several other means of a visitor obtaining shooting. Much commercial shooting is offered in conjunction with accommodation which ranges from self-catering in a humble but comfortable cottage to the luxury of a five-star hotel. Frequently it may be found that much of the best and most exciting pheasant shooting is leased in conjunction with accommodation in the grandest of aristocratic ancestral seats and historic castles. Indeed the visiting shooter might even find himself sleeping in a four-poster bed which was once graced by the eminent personage of King Edward VII.

Pheasant shooting in Scotland is not solely confined to formal driven shooting as a great deal of interesting and energetic sport may be had by 'walking-up'. This is usually conducted by a party of two to six guns walking in line through suitable cover behind a few questing spaniels which find and flush the game. Other species of game are also shot at the same time and this form of sport is referred to as rough or mixed shooting. This type of shooting normally produces far smaller bags than driven shooting and is therefore priced at a much lower level. Nevertheless such days may provide exhilarating sport and an interesting and varied bag. Chapter 12 deals with this aspect in full detail.

MODERN MANAGEMENT

Putting pheasants over the guns is a simpler process today. With modern systems and techniques a single keeper may produce more birds than ten of his Victorian counterparts. The production business still starts with the basic ingredient, the egg, but instead of searching for these in the wild, the modern keeper sets up a convenient production line on his doorstep. He catches up his stock of laying hens often during or soon after the closing month of the season in January and places them in small pens, one cock to six females. A useful labour-saving alternative, adopted by many single-handed keepers dealing with large numbers of birds, is the employment of an extensive communal pen with the same ratio of cocks to hens.

If manpower is limited, the estate will not attempt to incubate its own eggs but will utilise the services of a specialist game farm. These farms supply stock in the form of eggs, day-old chicks, six-week poults or adults. A common arrangement is for an estate to supply eggs to the farm and subsequently purchase six-week-old poults, the high cost of which will be offset by the value of eggs. In addition to its labour-saving benefits, this system enables the estate's resident stock to benefit from a healthy infusion of new blood each season. The keeper will have an established range of release pens in selected coverts around the estate and each will receive its quantity of poults delivered directly from the game farm.

The alternative that some estates opt for is the employment of their own incubation system where eggs are placed in machines which provide the right conditions for hatching. The subsequent day-old chicks are then transferred to a variety of brooding systems, all of which require specialised equipment and constant attention. Such a process is nerve-wracking for the keeper as many pitfalls may beset him. Power cuts, predators, adverse weather and a host of other misfortunes may lead to disaster. Whilst thus occupied the keeper is unable to devote time to reducing the numbers of pheasant predators on his ground. His more fortunate counterpart, who leaves the worries of incubation and poult raising to the game farm, has more time to attend to providing a safe environment for his young charges.

Clipping of the flight feathers in one wing is used to ensure that the young poults do not immediately fly out of the open-topped release pens. Following an acclimatisation period of two to three weeks the young bird goes through a moulting phase where the clipped wing feathers are cast and regrown and thus the birds gradually filter into the wild but are still enabled to return to the safety and food supply of their own pen. A cunning system of funnels and gates allows them back in but keeps large predators out. Thus they come to regard the wood containing their release pen as home and although they may forage out some distance during the day, most will normally return to roost and take delivery of next morning's breakfast. The keeper continues to provide feeding daily in their home coverts in order to discourage straying, especially on to neighbouring estates.

By this means the keeper ensures an even spread of birds throughout the various coverts on his ground and these will subsequently provide the main drives on shooting days. Most well–established estates were planted with conveniently placed woods intended principally as pheasant coverts and often strategically placed on high ground in order to present testing, high-flying birds. By late October the poults are virtually fully grown, becoming wild and strong on the wing. They are now in suitable fettle to receive their baptism of fire.

THE SHOOTING DAY

A typical day of formal driven pheasant shooting in Scotland is likely to go as follows. There will be a specified meeting place and time for the guns to assemble. On most pheasant shooting estates there will be a 'big house' which is normally the residence of the landowner and this would be the usual assembly point. It is quite normal and acceptable for guns to be accompanied by non-shooting family members or friends, but it is courteous to check first with host or agent to prevent problems with shoot transport and catering.

The standard time for arrival is 9 am. This allows time for guns to change into shooting clothing, have a cup of coffee, chat with fellow guns and meet their host who will circulate amongst them with a neat little leather wallet containing plastic tags. These, when drawn by each gun, reveal the number that designates their position on the first drive. Positions are indicated at the various drives by numbered pins marking where each gun is to stand. On most shoots there will be around eight guns and the pins are usually numbered from left to right whilst facing towards the drive. The standard practice is for each gun to move up two numbers each drive, ie, number two on the first drive would become number four on the second drive and, assuming there are eight guns, number eight would become number two. The system is designed to ensure that each gun has a chance of being in the best position at some stage during the day.

Moving off for the first drive usually takes place around 9.30 am. The estate will normally provide four-wheel drive transport but if the guns have suitable vehicles they may use their own for moving between drives. Should the guest guns have well-trained and well-behaved retrievers these are welcome but not essential. The guns will ensure that they have with them at each stand a full bag of cartridges, usually 100. Their reserve supply, which to be on the safe side should number at least 250, should travel with them.

Weapons are transported and carried to the pins in leather or canvas gun sleeves, which in addition to protecting valuable pieces, illustrate to the rest of the party that the gun is safely stowed. Obviously great care must be taken to ensure that guns remain unloaded at all times when they are not in immediate use.

Anticipating the start of the drive, the experienced shots stand quietly in their positions with guns loaded and ready but carried safely. They may be enjoying a quiet cigar but will not be conversing in loud tones with their neighbours. Pheasants have exceedingly good hearing and may be diverted in another direction altogether by noisy chatter.

The careful host will have pointed out to the guns the positions of any 'stops' who may be within firing range. These are members of the beating team who have been allocated the task of blocking possible exit routes from the main coverts. This helps to ensure that the birds do not stray prematurely from the wood or exit in the wrong direction in the course of a drive. There may be some feature of the drive like an overgrown ditch leading away from the front or side of the wood up which pheasants are likely to run. Stops will be positioned in such places.

The head keeper marshals his team of beaters to commence the drive and directs its progress, ensuring that a straight line is kept at all times. The team is likely to number about ten and is usually comprised of enthusiasts who enjoy a day out on the shoot. Although they do receive a small payment it is often the sport and comradeship that matter to them more than the money. It is curious how beating styles differ on various shoots and in different parts of the country. On the grand English estates the beat is inclined to be very orderly and refined. Beaters must remain silent. The only noise permitted during the drive is the tapping sound of sticks against trees as the line advances through the wood. Scottish pheasant flushing is generally a more jolly and robust affair and a wide range of motley calls, shouts, whistles and hoots may issue forth from the team as they push the birds out. Each bird that rises is greeted with enthusiastic cries which does help to provide an advance warning system to the guns.

On some shoots a whistle or a horn is blown to signify the start of the drive, but this is not always the case and guns should be prepared for the first 'Birds over!' that may arrive totally unannounced. Of far greater importance is the horn or whistle which is blown by the head keeper to signal the end of the drive, and it is mandatory that no shot is fired thereafter – no matter what tempting target may present itself. During his initial address to the guns, the host may well have mentioned that the normal rule is that no ground game is to be shot, ie hares or rabbits, and on no account must a gun shoot at any species of deer.

As the birds start to come over, the guns will be expected to shoot only those which present safe and sporting shots. Anything which flies at less than around 50 ft (16 m)

should be ignored and on no account should any low shot be taken either in front, sideways or behind. There are beaters in front, fellow guns to the side and pickers-up behind. It is accepted practice on formal shoots that anyone who infringes vital safety rules is immediately and permanently banished from the field. Anyone watching the line of guns in action may readily pick out experienced and expert shots by the fact that they invariably take their birds in front or directly overhead. They are rarely seen to wheel around and fire at a retreating bird.

Game is not retrieved by guns during the drive but guns do attempt to note numbers and positions of fallen birds. At some distance behind the line of guns several pickers-up will be placed. These are normally gundog enthusiasts who often have field trial class dogs which are a joy to watch. Although, like the beaters, they are paid for their work, the majority attend simply for the pleasure of working their dogs and joining in the day's sport. Top priority is to ensure that any birds wounded but not killed outright should be picked and dispatched as humanely and as quickly as possible. A winged pheasant is capable of running very fast and very far and if it is apparent that a picker-up has not noticed a runner, it is helpful if the guns bring it to their attention.

Those unfamiliar with gundog handling may expect that all shot pheasants, even when lying in full view in an open field, should be retrieved by a dog. In fact, the retriever's main job, in addition to securing runners, is to find, by scent, those birds which are lost to sight.

An experienced picker-up will often pick easily seen birds by hand, while their dogs remain seated. It is good practice for the guns to liaise with pickers-up after the drive to ensure that all shot birds are found. As an adult cock pheasant may weigh up to four pounds, considerate guns will assist the pickers-up in carrying the birds back to the game cart. Frequently the dogs continue to be worked after the guns have moved on and the pickers-up may arrive a little late at the next drive.

The second drive of the morning will normally finish around eleven o'clock, traditionally the time for a hot toddy or other beverage. A further two drives before lunch are normal, when the party will retire to the 'big house' or alternatively to a local hostelry. On a commercial shoot, lunch is normally included in the cost. After lunch a further two or three drives will bring the day's sport to a close.

The keepers and pickers-up will empty the game cart and hang birds in the game larder, where guns often congregate in order to comment on the day's bag and to thank the team for their efforts. If guests are staying overnight it is normal for the keeper to take charge of their guns, clean them and store them in the gun room. Before they depart the keeper will present each gun with a brace of birds and it is at this stage that the traditional tip is passed over. This often produces embarrassed uncertainty for the inexperienced. Guns may soon learn if they have been a trifle parsimonious. Their brace of 'grace' birds are likely to be the ones that the two badly trained retrievers fought over on the last drive. Failing such handy reprisals, inventive keepers have been known to give the gift brace a quick trample in the back of the game cart. Those shooting on a commercial day should consult with the agent or organiser as to the appropriate amount to tip. Invited guests will not be out of step if they tip at the rate of £10 per 100 birds shot.

Scottish custom and climate demand hot baths and large drams to complete the day.

LOCATIONS AND COSTS

Driven pheasant shooting is normally let by the day for a party of six to nine guns. The ancitipated bag is agreed beforehand, the most common number being a 200-bird day, which should give plenty of sport for everyone. The cost of the day is based on a per bird price multiplied by the total agreed anticipated bag. The price normally includes all transport on the shoot, all shoot staff, lunch and a complimentary brace of birds to each gun. The expected gratuities to the keepers are normally an additional cost. It is generally possible for the shoot organiser to manage the day so that the anticipated bag is achieved. Should there be a good class of shooting, a complimentary ten per cent over-run is often allowed and thereafter additional birds shot will be charged for at the going rate. If the standard of shooting is poor, parties should not necessarily expect to kill the agreed bag. The accepted standard of reasonable shooting is to kill one bird for every three shots. The headkeeper has a special counting device and will normally keep a tally of shots fired. This will be produced at the end of the day if required.

Pheasant shooting is the most reliable form of gameshooting and even in very adverse weather conditions it is normally possible to carry on with the proceedings. It is possible to take out bad weather shoot cancellation insurance and most sporting agents will arrange for this. Normally it is only in conditions of very deep snow, where transport and movement is severely hampered, that a pheasant shoot is likely to be cancelled. Some agents offer walked up pheasants which present a very acceptable low cost alternative to formal shooting. If properly carried out this can still offer some very good sport, particularly if another variety of game is included.

WILD PHEASANTS, the roughshooters' prize quarry. Ring-neck, melanistic and bohemian-type cocks. (*John Andrews*)

The prime areas for pheasant shooting are Perthshire, Angus, Morayshire, Aberdeenshire and Fife.

The following agencies will be pleased to arrange pheasant shooting for visiting guns.

Sport in Scotland Ltd

Driven pheasant shooting on several estates near Inverness and Perth. Generally these estates do not produce large numbers in the bag each day but the quality is very good – the birds fly high and fast. The preference is to provide 150-bird days but any size of day is catered for up to 250 birds. A team of eight guns is preferred but driven pheasant days for teams from two to ten may be arranged.

The price basically depends on the bag. A team expecting 150 birds will be charged £3,150. As a rule, good shots are allowed to shoot up to ten per cent above expectation before the shoot is stopped or a surcharge is instituted. The fee covers transport on the shoot, beaters, keepers, pickers-up and dogs and a brace of birds to each gun. Accommodation to suit the shooters' taste and pocket may be arranged.

Contact: Sport in Scotland Ltd, 22, Market Brae, Inverness, IV2 3AB. Tel: 0463 222757/232104. Telex 75446.

R F Watson, Scottish Sporting Agent

All types of pheasant shooting available throughout Scotland from best quality driven shoots to modest walked up days. Prices on application.

Contact: R F Watson, Scottish Sporting Agent, Jubilee Cottage, Fowlis Wester, Perthshire, PH7 3NL. Tel: 0764 83468. Fax: 0764 83475.

James Crockart & Sons, Blairgowrie

Formal driven pheasants and walked up shooting is available in Angus and Perthshire, including accommodation in Blairgowrie. Prices on application.

Contact: Robert Jamieson, James Crockart & Son, Allan Street, Blairgowrie, Perthshire, PH10 6AD. Tel: 0250 2056.

Alvie Estate

Pheasant shooting together with a variety of mixed game is available on the estate. Prices are available on application. Lodge and self-catering accommodation.

Contact: Nick Lewtas, Alvie Estate Office, Kincraig, Kingussie, Inverness-shire, PH21 1NE. Tel: 0504 255/249. Fax: 05404 380.

Invery House, Aberdeenshire

Driven and walked up pheasant shooting is available for hotel guests in the Deeside area. Driven £14.50 plus VAT/bird. Walked up £90 plus VAT/gun/day.

Contact: Stewart Spence, Invery House, Banchory, Royal Deeside, Kincardineshire, AB3 3NJ. Tel: 03302 4782. Telex: 73737. Fax: 03302 4712.

Cultoquhey House Hotel, Perthshire

Driven and walked up pheasant shooting available to hotel guests in Perthshire. Prices on application.

Contact: David Cooke, Cultoquhey House Hotel, Crieff, Perthshire, PH7 3NE. Tel: 0764 3253.

Scone Estates

Days of driven pheasants are available for parties of eight guns ranging from 400 plus birds at the start of the season to 150–200 at the end. There is a tremendous variety of drives on the estate, from formal coverts near the Palace to exciting bank shooting beside the river Almond. Price in the region of £6,000 plus VAT for a day of eight guns shooting 300 pheasants.

Contact: The Factor, Estates Office, Scone Palace, Perth, PH2 6BD. Tel: 0738 52308. Fax: 0738 52588.

John Andrews Sporting

Modest walked up days to best quality driven days in East Lothian, Perthshire and Angus. Walking days for two to six guns from £100 to £150 per gun/day. Driven days for parties of six to eight at around £15.50 per bird. Prices exclusive of VAT. Three- to six-day mixed shooting programmes and complete packages a speciality.

Contact: John Andrews, Muirside House, Bellies Brae, Kirriemuir, Angus, DD8 4EB. Tel: 0575 74350.

Major Neil Ramsay

Best quality driven days on prestigious estates in Perthshire and Angus. 150 to 300-bird days for seven to nine guns. From £16.50 to £19.50

per bird exclusive of VAT, including provision of sporting staff and transport on shoot.

Contact: Major Neil Ramsay, Tay Terrace, Dunkeld, Perthshire, PH8 OAQ. Tel: 03502 8991. Fax: 03502 8800.

Macsport Ltd

Quality driven birds on estates in Aberdeenshire, Kincardineshire, Angus and Fife. Specialise in complete packages including private country house accommodation. Hosted weekend shooting programmes. Normally around 200-bird days. Cost per bird around £14.50 plus VAT.

Contact: Macsport Ltd, Ballater Road, Aboyne, Aberdeenshire, AB3 5HT. Tel: 03398 86896. Fax: 03398 86291.

Tulchan Estate

Quality driven pheasants in the spectacular scenery of Speyside. Bags of two to three hundred birds. Accommodation in the fascinating Tulchan Lodge – a favourite sporting venue of King Edward VII.

Contact: Tim Kirkwood, Factor, Tulchan Estate, Grantown-on-Spey. Morayshire, PH26 3PW. Tel: 08075 200/261.

Tweed Valley Hotel, Peeblesshire

50 to 200-bird quality driven days for parties of six to eight guns in Peeblesshire. Prices on application. High bird clay shooting practice available in hotel grounds.

Contact: Charles Miller, Tweed Valley Hotel, Walkerburn, Peeblesshire, EH43 6AA. Tel: 089687 636. Fax: 089687 639.

Kildonan Hotel, Ayrshire

Driven and walked up pheasants available on the Drumlanford Estate in Ayrshire. Prices on application.

Contact: Iain Bibby, The Kildonan Hotel, Barrhill, Ayrshire. Tel: 0465 82360.

East Haugh House Hotel, Perthshire

Walked up pheasant shooting, including other game, available to guests of the hotel. Angus and Perthshire. Prices available on application.

Contact: East Haugh House, By Pitlochry, Perthshire, PH16 5JS. Tel: 0796 3121.

Fernie Castle Hotel, Fife

Driven and walked up pheasant available in Fife for hotel guests; walked up £100 plus VAT per person per day, driven (per bird divided by number of guns) £14 plus VAT, ie, 100 pheasant shot = £1,400 plus VAT, divided by eight guns = £175 plus VAT per gun.

Contact: Mr R Marsland, Fernie Castle Hotel, Letham, Near Cupar, Fife, KY7 7RU. Tel: 033781 381. Fax: 033781 422.

Lands of Loyal Hotel, Alyth

This long-established sporting hotel offers a range of driven and walked up pheasant shooting in Perthshire and Angus. Prices available on application.

Contact: Mr Howell, Lands of Loyal Hotel, Alyth, Perthshire, PH11 8JQ. Tel: 08283 3151. Fax: 08283 3313.

THE KEEPER collects eggs in the laying pen. (*John Andrews*)

8 The Partridge

CHANGED DAYS

TIME WAS WHEN this comely bird of field and furrow was the mainstay of British game shooting. The top-hatted and tail-coated sportsman of yesteryear eagerly anticipated the great day that signalled the start of the partridge shooting season – 1 September. *Perdix perdix*, the grey or English partridge, thrived in its millions in the weedy and insect-ridden farmland of the time with its patchwork of small enclosures separated by warm and welcoming hedgerows. The partridge reigned supreme as a gamebird throughout England and in most of the lowland counties of Scotland until the post-war revolution in agricultural practice began to destroy what was, for the partridge, an ideal habitat.

The bird had earned the greatest respect as a sporting quarry and was given the status almost of a lowland grouse. Shooting practices on the stubble fields and grass leas were carried out in a similar manner to grouse shooting, as the behaviour of the partridge lent itself to similar techniques. Thus driving and shooting over pointers were the methods practised most often. So significant was its place in the shooting scene of the time that even the rabbit, in the vast numbers of its pre-myxomatosis days, did not attract as much attention from the shotgun. In the early post-war years, the Eley Cartridge Company established that they sold more of their cartridges for partridge shooting than for any other quarry, and the total annual bag in the UK was estimated to be around 2 million.

In the 1950s government policies encouraged vast increases in agricultural output and so-called farming improvements changed the face of the land. Hedges were torn out, fields enlarged, insecticides and pesticides destroyed much of the partridge's favourite food. Numbers dropped significantly as the easily reared pheasant began to dominate the game shooting scene: partridge shooting on a major scale became a thing of the past. Fortunately there were men among the barley barons who would not relinquish the partridge as their favourite sporting bird and with encouragement from research organisations such as The Game Conservancy discovered ways in which modern agricultural practice and partridge production could be made compatible. One man who spearheaded this

JUST LIKE pheasants, redlegs may be held in covert by feeding. (*Roger Tidman*)

work was both an innovative, highly successful agriculturalist and owned some of the best partridge shoots in the country. Sir Joseph Nickerson proved conclusively by practical example that with restrained use of chemicals and good keepering techniques, modern farming could be both highly productive and co-exist happily with the development of a substantial partridge population. His efforts, coupled with the work of The Game Conservancy, has greatly encouraged landowners in following his outstanding example. On a few enlightened estates, the fortunes of the partridge have been somewhat restored and healthy coveys are now present in numbers reminiscent of times past.

Although some estates have had moderate success wich rearing the grey partridge it does not readily lend itself to artificial production. In the late eighteenth century the French or red-legged partridge was introduced from Europe. Although not a particularly enthusiastic flyer, when presented properly the red-leg does provide a sporting target, but to devotees it does not compare with the native wild bird. The red-leg's great saving grace is that it is easily reared in large numbers and with a bit of encouragement not over inclined to wander from its release area. Therefore estates which provide commercial partridge days with reared birds are inclined to stock with French rather than grey partridge. The foreigners have successfully established themselves in the wild and even on shoots which do not rear partridge, wild 'Frenchies' make an occasional and welcome addition to the bag.

THE NATURE OF THE BIRD

Most sporting and country folk have a greater affection for the partridge than any other bird. No other creature quite captures the spirit of couthie rural life in lowland farming areas. Part of the appeal of this homely bird is its impeccable respectability and admirable devotion to family life. Unlike that rakish philanderer, the cock pheasant, and his hen, an incompetent mother at best, partridge pair for life and are exemplary parents.

Being territorial by nature, by late April the partridge pair will have selected their nesting area and the cock bird will defend it vigorously against intrusion by encroaching neighbours. This is in sharp contrast to its gregarious habit of winter. Prospective parent partridges seek to rear their offspring in privacy and cannot bear to be within sight of another partridge pair. This temporary lack of sociability is Nature's way of ensuring an even population density and an equable share of available food supplies.

Hedgerows are greatly favoured as nest sites and by early June most hen birds will be cosily installed on top of a clutch of 15 to 20 eggs. Meanwhile her faithful consort will stand guard and join her in parental duties when the chicks hatch in three weeks' time. Both parents are courageous and will attempt to drive off any intruder no matter how large, either by a straight attack or by the subterfuge of flapping off, apparently incapacitated, drawing the danger on themselves. No chauvinist, the cock partridge takes its share of parental duties, helping to shelter and brood the chicks in bad weather and at night. Chicks are ready to leave the nest and feed themselves almost as soon as they are hatched, accompanying their parents who shepherd them around the territory while they search for food.

It is at this stage that the chicks are most vulnerable, because they can fall victim to cold and wet. It is also essential that they have a plentiful supply of insects to ensure that they thrive, so the farmer who has wisely left unsprayed headlands in his cereal crops is rewarded by an additional crop of game.

The covey will stay together until autumn when the rigours of the shooting season may split up the family group. Individual birds may then join together in larger groups for the winter before pairing off in spring to seek territories of their own.

THE FLAWCRAIG EXPERIENCE

Not far to the north of the A85 Perth to Dundee road lies the small hamlet of Rait. Close to Rait is Flawcraig which is both a gamefarm and a very unusual partridge shoot. The proprietor of Flawcraig is Peter Leslie, a partridge expert if ever there was one. Peter produces many thousands of partridge, pheasant and duck to stock shoots all over the country but his speciality is partridge – the native grey, French red-legged, chucker and a variety of crosses.

Flawcraig is situated in an unusual situation. From the flat Carse of Gowrie, adjacent to the Tay estuary, a wooded escarpment rises sharply from 50 ft (15 m) above sea level to over 800 ft (244 m) looking down on the ancient Fingask Castle. After establishing the gamefarm some years ago, Peter soon discovered that this warm south facing escarpment and surrounding arable ground was the type of terrain that is remarkably well-suited to all species of partridge. He expanded his area of shooting rights and started to build up what is probably the most productive and challenging driven partridge shoot in Scotland, one which could rival most of the top English partridge manors.

Apart from the obvious necessity of a good stock of birds, the main requirement for a first-class driven partridge shoot is suitable cover to hold the birds and to drive them from. To start with, Flawcraig had a good network of small mixed woodlands and useful areas of rough scrubby cover, and these areas have been much extended by planting many blocks of game crop. The most successful game crop that Peter has found for his partridge is a combination of quinoa and thousand-head kale. The quinoa will grow to almost 6 ft (2 m) and produces a seed head very similar to millet, thus providing both ideal cover and attractive feeding for partridge. The quinoa does gradually become laid over the season, but when it is surrounded by the kale it receives protection and the whole gamecrop becomes both a warm haven and an enticing foraging area for both partridge and pheasant. By the use of this crop the holding capacity of the ground has been enormously increased and these blocks permit a variety of drives to be carried out on a shooting day by a complicated, but highly efficient, series of blanking-in manoeuvres.

A day of driven partridge at Flawcraig is a spectacular event. Parties of five to seven guns are catered for and bags of 300 to 500 are available. There can be few other such places that are able to arrange consistently to have that level of partridge production. Guns of varying ability are catered for. None of the birds is easy and could probably be classified as average, difficult, very difficult and nearly impossible. One of the many impressive features of a Flawcraig day is that guns are not obliged to spend a deal of time in the transport, moving laboriously from one drive to another. The estate is compact and the drives are cleverly arranged to ensure that the party is able to move rapidly from one set of stands to another. No waiting about for half an hour with frozen feet here.

There are few shoots where guns may remain at the same stand for a full hour and have a variety of partridge coming over at all angles throughout that time. Full use is made of the escarpment to present partridge at a height and speed that will thrill and test to the full the most expert and seasoned gameshot. Such artistry in game presentation is brought about by a high level of management and expertise by a man who not only knows his profession intimately but who also retains an enormous and infectious enthusiasm for providing the very best of sporting occasions for his guests.

After a morning of superb sport, lunch at Flawcraig is a delight in itself. High up above the vast and scenic sweep of the Tay estuary, looking far out to the North sea and way across to the hills of Fife, sits the superbly

sited estate farmhouse where lunch is served. The view is breathtaking and so is the lunch. Peter states that the ratio of kills to cartridges invariably deteriorates in the afternoon.

Flawcraig is a remarkable place and to shoot these high altitude partridge is a unique and memorable experience. Following a drive from the highest point of the escarpment on a day of strong wind, a seasoned old keeper from Aberdeenshire turned to Peter with the remark,

'Man, that was just grand. Thae birds is o'er three gunshots too high!'

Parties wishing to sample the Flawcraig experience should contact Peter A Leslie, Flawcraig Game Farm, Rait, Perthshire. Tel: Rait (08217) 306.

LOCATIONS AND COSTS

Specialised partridge shooting and days when partridge only are the quarry are not too easy to come by in Scotland. Such shooting is inclined to be more readily available in England, as in the southern counties there are a good number of estates that have specialised for over 100 years as 'partridge manors'. However, many days of mixed shooting in Scotland will include a fair number of partridge in the bag. For days of exclusive partridge shooting, the following suppliers will readily be of assistance.

The average price per bird at 1990 prices was approximately £15.50 for driven partridge and around £90 per gun/day for walked up birds, including VAT at 15 per cent.

Macsport Ltd

Partridge shooting in Aberdeenshire and Angus.
Driven – £15.50 plus VAT per bird.
Walked up – £90 plus VAT per gun/day.
Over dogs – £90 plus VAT per gun/day plus cost of dogs.

   Contact: Macsport Ltd, Ballater Road, Aboyne, Aberdeenshire, AB3 5HT. Tel: 03398 86898. Fax: 03398 86291.

Invery House, Aberdeenshire

Partridge shooting – either driven, walked up or over dogs – is available for hotel guests at the following prices:
Driven – £15.50 plus VAT per bird.
Walked up – £90 plus VAT per gun/day.
Over dogs – £190 plus VAT per gun/day.

   Contact: Stewart Spence, Invery House, Banchory, Royal Deeside, Kincardineshire, AB3 3NJ. Tel: 03302 4782. Telex: 73737. Fax: 03302 4712.

Fernie Castle Hotel

The hotel arranges partridge shooting for its guests in Fife. Cost is £100 plus VAT per person per day.

   Contact: Mr R Marsland, Fernie Castle Hotel, Letham, Near Cupar, Fife, KY7 7RU. Tel: 033781 381. Fax: 033781 422.

John Andrews Sporting

Walked up partridge over pointers and driven grey and redleg in East Lothian, Angus and Perthshire. Price dependent on bag required.

   Contact: John Andrews Sporting, Muirside House, Bellie's Brae, Kirriemuir, Angus, DD8 4EB. Tel: 0575 74350. Fax: 0575 72399.

SIKA STAGS from East Sutherland, a cull beast on the left and two mature stags on the right. (*Sport in Scotland*)

A GOOD retriever is essential for wildfowling. (*John Andrews*)

9 The Oddball Grouse

IN ADDITION TO the 'famous grouse' there are three other members of the grouse family which are indigenous to Scotland. All are currently legal quarry and have their own peculiarities and preferred habitat.

CAPERCAILLIE

This magnificent bird's name comes from the Gaelic, meaning 'cock of the woods'. The capercaillie (*Tetrao urogallus*) is by far the largest member of the grouse family, the cocks standing 33 to 35 in (84 to 89 cm) high and the hens at 23 to 25 in (58 to 64 cm). The cock is dark blue/black overall with a glossy blue/green breast, it has a massive head with a substantial curved beak, patriarchal beard-like feathering under its chin and a distinctive red patch around the eye. The cock may weigh anything from 9 to 12 lb (4 to 5 kg). The large feet of the species have a unique toe conformation, with the hind toe being strongly curved and set against the others to provide a secure locking arrangement which gives the bird complete security when roosting in high firs on stormy nights. The toes are pectinated, being slightly rough toothed giving the ability to clamber up and down with ease on slippery branches in the treetops. It has a large broad tail which it displays turkey-fashion in the breeding season. The hen is rather dowdy by comparison, looking for all the world like an overgrown hen grouse. She is little more than half the cock's weight, her feathers being barred with white, light and dark brown.

The cock 'caper' is a real exhibitionist in the spring as, in addition to a tail displaying technique to impress his chosen hen, he often installs himself on a prominent tree branch and broadcasts his love-lilt to the world at large. At such times the cock appears almost to go into a state of trance. His popping, burbling call is jointly a means of attracting hens, declaring his territorial rights to an area of woodland and announcing the droit de seigneur on his admiring harem to any rivals within earshot. The capercaillie is a pugnacious bird at the best of times and never more so than in the breeding season. Quite vicious battles for females and territory take place, and so bold do some individuals become that it is not unknown for them to attack humans. For several years there was one notorious individual in Rothiemurchus Forest that went to the extreme of attempting to knock seven bells out of highly polished motor cars. Presumably it was his own reflection that prompted the aggression and not a pathological hatred of the internal combustion engine.

The courtship habits of the magnificent male of the species do it little favour in some parts of Scandinavia. Normally a bird that is very wary and difficult to approach when in the treetops, the caper's natural reserve is overcome in springtime by his lust for females and territory. Rather unsportingly, the wicked Swedes take advantage of his preoccupation at this time and delight in blasting him off his perch with a rifle. Not the sort of ploy that a Scottish sporting gentleman would indulge in.

The bird's preferred habitat is the mature coniferous woodland of upland areas and, rather appropriately, it is particularly fond of Scots pine woods. It spends a good deal of its time in summer on the ground where it also nests, and in winter it is mostly found in the tree-tops from which it takes off with a remarkable commotion when disturbed.

Capercaillie became extinct in Britain around 1760, but happily the species was re-introduced to Scotland from Sweden in the period 1837–8 by the Marquis of Breadalbane and Sir Thomas Fowell Buxton working in conjunction with Mr Lloyd, a naturalist. The initial stock was released at Kenmore in Perthshire and to commemorate the event a bronze bust of a cock capercaillie was commissioned. This can still be seen today in its stance on the roof of Kenmore Primary School.

Following this re-introduction the 'caper' spread and thrived throughout Scotland. Sadly its numbers did receive a set-back between the wars due to the wholesale clear felling of many of the large mature stands of Scots pine.

In Scotland the main concentrations of the capercaillie population are found in Perthshire, Angus, Moray and Aberdeenshire and there is a small population on the islands of Loch Lomond. Glasgow day-trippers often report seeing 'wild turkeys' flying from one island to another. There is a well-established population within a mile south of Perth city centre where they may be seen, on occasion, in stubble fields adjoining the A9.

Moderate 'caper' shooting does take place on some estates where there are good numbers, but such shoots are very limited and confined to cock birds only which now have a 'trophy' status. The usual method is to drive blocks of woodland quietly to standing guns. The flight of the capercaillie is very deceptive as, like most large birds, it is actually travelling at a far greater speed than it appears. A fast swing and a good lead are necessary. When waiting for birds to come forward in a drive the guns must be extremely vigilant. Unlike pheasants there is seldom an audible warning of the caper's approach. Although he will take off from high in a lofty Scots pine with the most alarming clatter, the bird's flight thereafter is often as silent as an owl. Guns are frequently caught out by this characteristic, and for many would-be trophy hunters a brief glimpse over the shoulder of a large, swift and silently departing black missile is the nearest that they will get. 'That was a capercaillie, that was!'

Early in 1990 the Government's Minister for the Environment at the Scottish Office was expressing concern over declining numbers of this attractive species and seeking views on a proposed national shooting ban. A ban had been introduced previously on all Forestry Commission estates in 1986. The Game Conservancy put forward the view that the sporting interest was essential to habitat management and predation control, pointing out that there was no evidence to link the capercaillie decline to overshooting, and stressing that many estates were already exercising a voluntary restraint. The Conservancy called on the Government to co-ordinate and fund research on capercaillie management rather than introduce a ban on shooting and was able to show that the population figures on which the Scottish Office had based its proposal were in fact somewhat flawed. The Conservancy's view and recommendations were endorsed by the British Association for Shooting and Conservation, the British Fieldsports Society and the Scottish Landowners' Federation.

The welcome outcome of this representation was that the Government announced that the shooting ban proposal had been dropped and that instead the Government would be assisting in establishing the necessary research. This change of heart on the Government's part is a significant precedent. Had capercaillie shooting been banned simply because it appeared that the species was in decline it could easily have come about that such a ban on shooting could have been introduced for blackgame, grey partridge and brown hares. These species have shown clear evidence of some decline in population levels in recent years. It has been clearly established that this decline has not been brought about by overshooting but is largely due to a number of environmental factors. Fortunately the government has now recognised the value of the sporting incentive in the conservation of a quarry species, its habitat and the other forms of wildlife which share it.

BLACKGAME

Also known as black grouse (*Lyrurus tetrix*) this very handsome bird is the source of the lyre-shaped plume so proudly worn in the hat badge of some famous Highland regiments. The blackcock is a glorious glossy black bird with white wing bars and a prominent red comb above the eye. Its distinctive black tail feathers have pronounced white under-feathers which become highly visible when the bird displays its tail during the courtship ritual. This may be quite a prolonged affair as the cock birds will start to gather on the traditional 'lekking' ground as early as December. They are not joined by the females (greyhens) until the early spring when the serious displays start. The greyhen is a smaller, fork-tailed bird, warm brown above and with paler under parts, mottled and barred with black throughout.

The favoured blackcock 'leks' are usually flat grassy areas situated among the heather and rushes of low moorland or marginal hill ground. Such gathering places, if they have not been altered or unduly disturbed have, in many cases, been habitually used by blackgame certainly for decades, if not centuries. Most of the ritual activity normally takes place in the early morning but birds may be seen on these 'leks' at any time of day. When the greyhens begin to join the blackcocks in the spring, the previous rather solemn and sedate all-male gatherings start to take on a different atmosphere. The party really begins to liven up as the males strut and posture, puffing out their chests and every possible part of their plumage. With tails erect, flashing their white behinds, wings drooping on the ground and necks extended in aggression, the cocks attempt to establish their power and superiority in order to win the hearts and minds of the attendant, somewhat bored-looking, greyhens. (Very similar behaviour may be witnessed among young humans frequenting Saturday nightclubs!)

There is a great deal of suitable habitat for this species in Scotland as blackgame prefer the moorland edge and marginal ground, having a preference for scattered groups of scrubby trees with adjacent wetlands, heather, rough arable land and grazing. It is a gregarious bird throughout the year and large winter flocks of 20 or 30 may sometimes be seen conspicuously perched in the slender branches of silver birch trees. It is found on marginal ground and moorland all over Scotland, with the biggest concentrations occuring in Perthshire, Angus, Morayshire and Inverness-shire. One of the most easily seen 'lekking' grounds is right beside the A826 Strathbraan to Aberfeldy road as it follows the line of General Wade's military road through Glen Cochill. The 'lek' is in the small grassy field on the left of the road heading north to Aberfeldy, just after the road crosses the bridge over the Cochill burn and before arriving at Scotston farm on the left. As many

as 25 blackcock may be seen here of an early morn from December to April.

A relevant plus factor in the survival and continuance of good population levels of blackgame is the huge variety in its diet. It feeds chiefly on plant material throughout the year and will take the opportunity of any nearby accessible grain crops. It may often be seen taking advantage of grain stubbles close by moorland areas and it will feed avidly on ripe blaeberries in early autumn. Many old oil paintings show great gatherings of blackgame and grouse on the oat stooks of the time which clearly provided very easy pickings for them. Their summer diet includes shoots and leaves of ground plants including good young heather, seeds, berries and some insect material. Apart from their forays on to any available grain stubbles, the winter diet consists chiefly of shoots and buds of birch and scots pine. It is the latter eating habit that has made this bird an enemy of the old-style foresters.

The old school of forestry encouraged among its practitioners a fanatical hatred of any creature that had the temerity to dare to nibble any little part of any one of their precious trees. It is astonishing to realise that, up until very recently, State employees of the National Forestry Commission were instructed to destroy all blackgame in State forests by whatever means possible. This included the immediate destruction of any eggs or nestlings that the forestry 'trapper' could discover. At that time vast tracts of Scotland were disappearing under endless blankets of alien conifers and the blackgame population suffered

extreme reductions in many areas through these policies. The Caledonian forest and large stocks of blackgame co-existed happily in centuries past, which does perhaps indicate that silviculture and blackgame are not necessarily incompatible. Happily, forestry policies are now somewhat more enlightened in their attitude to all forms of wildlife but the relentless march of the sterile Sitka spruce continues to smother much of Scotland's open hill.

Blackgame are much slower in maturing than red grouse and although their statutory season opens on 20 August, birds of the year are never anywhere near full grown by that date. It is grossly unfair to raise a gun at them much before October. To cut down young blackgame as they flutter up from the rushy hollows on a late August day during a walked up grouse shoot is a thoroughly reprehensible practice. Even adult birds are better left until later in the season when they will have had a chance to develop their full magnificent plumage. By October the birds will be worthy of the sportsman's attention and one or two cock birds, a few grouse and perhaps a hill partridge or two will make a most memorable day. Blackgame are often shot by chance during grouse shoots, but in some favoured areas, where there are substantial concentrations of the bird, specific blackgame drives are organised. The bird is more nervous than the red grouse and is not so readily approached when walking up, apart from early in the season. On grouse drives where blackgame occur it may be noted that their speed is greater than that of the grouse, although their wing-beat appears much slower.

In recent years there has been a demand for blackcock trophy hunting in the Continental manner when shooters, using .22 rifles, will attempt to stalk blackcock perched in trees. Perhaps a little alien to the Scottish sporting style, unlike some parts of Scandinavia, at least this method must be confined to the statutory blackgame season and it is restricted to the male of the species.

PTARMIGAN

The smallest member of the grouse family, the ptarmigan (*Lagopus mutus*) is a bird of high altitudes, seldom seen below 1,500 ft (457 m) except in very severe winter weather. Its most notable characteristic is its ability to turn virtually pure white in winter with the exception of its black tail and scarlet supra-orbital comb. The ptarmigan is the only bird in the UK that is able to change the colouration of its plumage to provide additional comouflage to suit seasonal conditions. The only other forms of British wildlife which have a similar ability are the mountain hare and the stoat. In summer, the cock bird is a dark greyish brown with light grey wings and the female is browner with tawny markings and light grey wings. The ptarmigan owes much to its plumage for concealment from its enemies, which are chiefly the hill fox and the golden eagle. Like grouse they are quite sociable birds preferring to remain in family coveys up until the spring.

This hardy little gamebird of the highest tops has a trusting nature and at times may be

IN THE butts on Speyside. (*Sport in Scotland*)

very easily approached, particularly once it gets used to the presence of humans. It may be seen frequently sporting itself among the skiers on the slopes at Cairngorm. It would appear that these 'civilised' birds which hang around the ski area have developed a taste for discarded hamburgers, potato crisps and other detritus of the winter sports scene. The normal

ESSENTIAL AID for the roughshooter – a good gundog. (*John Andrews*)

diet for the pure and clean-living ptarmigan is comprised almost entirely of plant matter such as shoots, leaves and berries of heathland plants. When extra-severe weather eventually drives the birds down to the lower slopes, they may resort to perching in the scrub birch to feed on buds, twigs and seeds. They are able to cope well with reasonably heavy snow as they will happily tunnel down several feet to find vegetation. Their distribution is confined largely to areas over 2,000 ft (610 m) in Ross-shire, Inverness-shire and Sutherland.

Ptarmigan shooting is a recognised sport but it is never carried out with the expectation of anything like a large bag. It is done more as a novelty – the experience of hunting an unusual and elusive quarry in dramatic surroundings. Ptarmigan shooters must be extremely fit, constantly on the alert and slightly masochistic. There are recognised 'ptarmigan hills', areas where ptarmigan have been found for centuries. It often takes a two to three-hour walk just to reach a potential ptarmigan hill. The word 'hill' is a bit of a misnomer, most ptarmigan-favoured areas are more approaching mountain size. After prolonged plodding and stumbling around the mountain the shooter may catch sight of a covey on some high ledge of the hill, scuttling about among the stones. With trepidation, the eager sportsman will approach the spot certain that the birds have not flown, yet when he climbs to the place to look for them among the lichen-clad granite there is not a bird to be seen. Cursing with frustration he will turn to retrace his steps, thinking that the birds have obviously slipped away round the side of the

hill. Another step and suddenly right in front of his feet a handful of greyish stones take the shape of birds and hurl themselves out from the mountain, far down into the abyss below before the gun has even found its way to the shoulder. With elusive and difficult shooting such as this a gun will have done well if a brace of birds is obtained for the day. Part of his reward will be that the birds are very tasty as well as making memorable and distinctive mounted trophies.

LOCATIONS AND COSTS

There are few suppliers who specifically offer sport solely concerned with any of the above species, although Sport in Scotland Ltd do offer specialised opportunities to shoot ptarmigan and blackgame. Three main ptarmigan shooting areas are available, one in Ross-shire, one in Sutherland and one in Inverness-shire. The price is £120 per gun per day, inclusive of VAT.

This company also provide blackcock trophy hunting near Dunkeld in Perthshire. The cost per hunter is £529 per week inclusive of accommodation and VAT. It is possible that other opportunities for driven and walked up blackcock may be available on request.

Contact: Sport in Scotland Ltd, 22, Market Brae, Inverness, IV2 3AB. Tel: 0463 222757/ 232104. Telex: 75446.

Limited driven and walked up blackcock shooting may be arranged in the Angus area by Robert Jamieson of James Crockart & Son, Allan Street, Blairgowrie, Perthshire, PH10 6AD. Tel: 0250 2056.

LOCH FASKALLY, Perthshire. (*Perthshire Tourist Board*)

WIDGEON FLOCK in flight over the Dornoch Firth. (*Roger Tidman*)

A SUSPICIOUS pinkfoot approaches the artificial decoys. (*John Andrews*)

SHOVELER DRAKE. (*Roger Tidman*)

TEAL DRAKE. (*Roger Tidman*)

GADWALL (DRAKE). (*Roger Tidman*)

HINDS ON the horizon. (*Sport in Scotland*)

STAG IN winter. (*Neil McIntyre*)

A MAGNIFICENT Royal in full winter coat. (*Neil McIntyre*)

E NVIRONMENTALLY FRIENDLY stag transport. (*Aaron Pass*)

A UCHNAFREE. (*Perthshire Tourist Board*)

A BUCK with a very long head in winter coat. Note the highly visible white rump. (*Sport in Scotland*)

A PROMISING wild billy goat: Given a few years this beast should produce a superb trophy head. (*Neil McIntyre*)

EVENING IS a convenient time to seek a summer roebuck. (*Perthshire Tourist Board*)

GLEN TILT.
(*Perthshire Tourist Board*)

10 Wildfowl

THE RETURN

SOMETHING STAYED THE angler's hand.

The crimson speckled golden body of the largest brown trout he had ever caught writhed within the folds of his landing net. His heart still pumped madly – the fish must have weighed all of four pounds.

The faint, almost recognised, sound intruded on his triumph. Hand still raised for the final blow, he turned his head from side to side striving to hear again. The vast Sutherland silence contained only the slap of waves against timber as his boat drifted in the light September wind. Yet still he paused.

Above the summit of Fashven, high and wild it came again. Now he knew it. A reminder of the well-loved sound of winter dawn on distant Lowland firths. Looking up he spied the great skeins. Anticipating pleasures yet to come, the wooden priest dropped from his hand. With gentle respect the prize trout was lifted over the gunwale and slipped back into the limestone-rich water.

Half a mile above the lonely Cape Wrath loch the forerunners of the massive autumn invasion of pinkfeet flung excited falsetto cries from skein to skein as they sighted the first landfall since leaving Iceland.

An hour later, as evening deepened over Dornoch Firth, the aged ploughman feebly struggled to raise his head from the pillow. Through the open window of the crumbling bothy by the shore came at last the music he had waited on to hear. He had worked this land of Ross for most of his 92 years – a lifetime that had seen much change. But one thing was constant. Always, his geese came back at the same time every year. Far out on the Whiteness sands the calling faded and died as the last gander whiffled down, thankfully tucking its head under a weary wing.

Old Rab also slept. Now he was content.

A hundred and twenty miles south, as dusk spread across the fat barley stubbles of a Perthshire estate, the laird's ten-year-old son swore as he swatted at the evening's maraud of midges. He was trying to keep still, his bare knees vulnerable and sore from kneeling on the harsh vegetation that surrounded the marshy haugh alongside the River Earn. His nervous sweaty hands clutched tightly at the aristocratic Boss sidelock. He strained his ears longing to hear the approaching chatter of duck. He desperately wanted to shoot a fat mallard – he had watched them the previous evening from his bedroom window flighting into this pond.

He had good reason to be nervous. The Boss belonged to his elder brother who had spent the afternoon shooting pigeons on the laid wheat. Anxious to meet his girlfriend in Perth, the gun had been carelessly abandoned in the Land-rover. Alexander could not believe his good fortune; there were even plenty of cartridges. His father was safely out of the way, driving one of the combines in an attempt to clear the last remaining acreage of barley whilst the weather held. He could see the machine's headlights way up on the high ground. This was his chance and he would endure the penance of the midges.

The cries of the approaching pinkfeet were unexpected and thrilling. His ambition soared as he thrust himself flat among the rushes. He knew the geese sometimes came here at night when the winter rains flooded the low lying land. He shivered violently with anticipation as the far off clamour grew closer. His inexperience could not identify the calls as pinkfeet – they never came here. This was a roost for greylags which were as yet far away and would not migrate to Scotland until late October.

Alexander squinted with disdain at the five mallard that swept over his recumbent body to land at the far side of the pond. He yearned only for the grand prize now.

High above, the pinks swept on to cross the Ochil hills, breaking into joyful clamour as, through the dusk, they sighted the watery gleam of their winter home.

Willie Wilson, fishery manager on Loch Leven, paused as he closed up the boathouse for the night. Out in the darkness, way over the island of St Serfs he heard the jubilant chatter of their arrival.

Willie smiled with pleasure as he turned the key. The first of his winter friends were back.

THE GREY GEESE

Of all the birds and beasts of the chase our wild grey geese inspire the greatest passion and fanaticism in those who are true hunters and not just live target shooters. This incongruous mixture of respect, genuine affection and yet desire to pursue the quarry is also to be found among salmon anglers.

Perhaps this charismatic attraction that both species hold for the sportsman has some basis in the mystery of their movements. Both fish and fowl range unfettered throughout their respective elements of air and water. Both are transient seasonal visitors to these islands, travelling to our shores over incredible distances. Both species have beauty, strength, nobility and a true wildness. Both require skill, experience and fieldcraft if consistent success is to be achieved in their pursuit. The wild goose and the salmon feature prominently in folklore and mythology – creatures that are here today and gone tomorrow. Both stir the heart and mind of man the hunter.

The two main species of grey geese that winter in Scotland are the greylag (*Anser anser*) and the pink-footed (*Anser brachyrhynchus*). The larger of the two species, the greylag, breeds in Iceland, Scandinavia and Central Europe, but only those which breed in Iceland migrate to the UK in winter. Greylags arrive

in late October or November and leave again in March or April staying for a shorter time than the pink-footed. There is a minor resident population of greylags in Scotland which breed in the Outer Hebrides and a small flock remain and breed in the Loch Tummel area of Perthshire. The pink-footed goose breeds in a different area of Iceland and also in east Greenland, arriving in Scotland from mid-September and departing in late April to mid-May. Other species of geese which occur as winter migrants are the Greenland white-fronted, the bean and the barnacle, all of which are protected in Scotland and of no interest as quarry species. Overwintering populations number around 90,000 greylags and 100,000 pinkfeet and the overall numbers appear to be on the increase for both species. The great black and white Canada goose has a feral population in Scotland, now well-established, which is on the increase. They are legal quarry and are shot by sportsmen on occasion. Considerable flocks have established themselves in the Moray Firth and in west Perthshire.

Both main quarry species, greylags and pinkfeet, are inclined to favour the east coast of Scotland and their main wintering areas are Perthshire, Kinross, Angus and Fife. The two species do not normally mix and are inclined to occupy quite separate feeding and roosting areas. Geese have a different regime from duck, feeding by day and roosting at night. At times of bright moonlight this habit may change when they will sometimes flight under the moon to their feeding grounds. On their arrival in autumn they favour feeding on the

grain stubbles and later in the year will turn their attention to potato and grass fields. Given the opportunity, they develop a great liking for gleaning carrot fields. With the increase in winter-sown cereals the geese frequently become most unpopular with farmers, as they are inclined to descend on this succulent new growth in early spring and may do considerable damage.

Favoured roosting areas for both species are the large firths or estuaries on the east coast. Notable among these are the Eden and Tay estuaries, the Montrose Basin, the Moray and Dornoch Firths. The sole major west coast roost is the Solway Firth. In addition the grey geese use a number of inland freshwater roosts from hill lochs and reservoirs to flooded fields. Loch Leven in Kinross is one of the most notable inland roosts. Geese will, on occasion, remain and roost on their feeding grounds but normally there is considerable movement to and fro at dawn and evening, when most serious goose shooting is done. Where geese find ample feed, such as a newly harvested potato field, which is a particular favourite of pinks, their numbers will build up to several thousand on this ground for as long as the food lasts and provided that they are not seriously disturbed. When numbers like this lift off the field in the evening, heading for some distant roost, the sight is quite awesome.

SHOOTING METHODS

To those who would pursue the wild goose, several options are open. There is a breed of wildfowler that regards all forms of inland goose shooting as unsporting and fit only as a pursuit for 'wimps'. Such macho characters probably take cold showers in the morning and also wear hair shirts.

These purists pursue their sport from the saltings and foreshore of the major firths seeking their shot whilst chill dawn breaks and the great grey birds flight from salt-swept sandbars to feed inland. At dusk they may again be found crouching in pain and discomfort in some coastal muddy gutter as winter winds do blow and icy rain descends, seeking to ambush the birds on their return. This manly sport offers romance, tradition, heart-stopping excitement, frustration, suffering and danger. Designer-built for masochists, it is highly addictive and draws unfortunate addicts from their beds at an ungodly hour of dawn.

Concealment on the foreshore is often a major problem and the coastal fowler has to be an opportunist, taking advantage of any form of cover and even in extreme cases lying flat on his back in the open. Shooting from such a position requires skill of an unusual degree and a sense of humour is a great advantage as it does seem ludicrous to lie out on the open shore in the middle of winter looking like a dead body, waiting for geese to fly by. Those of a more energetic disposition may take a shovel with them and 'dig in'. This is an art in itself and requires familiarisation with normal flight-lines. Local knowledge of the area and tides is essential for success and safety – visitors are recommended to seek the services of a local guide. Coastal fowling can be an extremely dangerous pursuit due to the speed with which the tide may gallop in on the shallow estuaries.

It used to be fashionable for shore shooters to use large bore guns – 8 bores and 10 bores were in common use and for the more heroic gunner a single barrel 4 bore, firing up to a shoulder stomping 4 oz (113 g) of shot, might be the chosen weapon. (A double 4 bore would be too much, even for a Goliath.) With these cumbersome arms great weights of shot could be blasted into the air and it was commonly thought that the more ounces of shot that could be put up the greater was the chance of it making a fatal connection with a high flying goose. The major problem with these big bores was the sheer effort required to transport them around on the hazardous shore as some would weigh in the region of 15 lb (7 kg). It was difficult to initiate sufficient momentum with these heavyweights when trying to swing on to a bird and difficult to stop it once it was underway. Many an eager big bore fancier has found himself carried earthwards to fall flat on his back in the mud as he tried to swing his mini-cannon on to a high overhead goose. The efficient powders and loads for today's magnum 12 bores have now rendered these ponderous arms obsolete. The high cost and difficulty of obtaining cartridges has also helped to seal their fate and these days only eccentric enthusiasts will be found using the redoubtable old 4, 8 and 10 bores.

The wildfowler who intends to specialise in seeking his geese below the high water mark would be best served by a 3 in magnum 12 bore, proofed for the maximum load of 1⅞ oz. Although such a load will enable clean kills to be made on geese at up to 60 yd (55 m), this is a very long shot and few people are capable of sufficient accuracy to be able to use this weapon to its full potential. For big strong birds like geese it is a humane policy to be rather over than under-gunned, provided that the magnum is not seen as some kind of magic wand and fired at birds at extreme range. The subject of shot sizes for geese has provided endless controversy but most experienced fowlers will opt for 3, 1 or BB shot. Anything larger is inclined to throw very erratic patterns and will not produce consistent clean kills.

The inland fowler may have an easier time than his rugged counterpart on the coast but even then a certain amount of skill and fieldcraft is required if success is to be achieved. It certainly must be said that shooting geese over decoys on their feeding grounds may at times be very easy indeed and unfortunately some shocking slaughters by greedy and unscrupulous gunners have taken place. Although on occasion crop protection is put forward as an excuse for such mass murder there is no justification whatsoever for this avaricious and irresponsible behaviour.

When conducted in a reputable and sporting manner, shooting a moderate bag of geese inland is a legitimate and respectable pursuit. The three main ways in which this is conducted are decoying, driving and flighting.

Decoying is a popular and effective method and is frequently used by professional wildfowling guides. It involves the use of a considerable amount of equipment comprising hide, an adequate supply of decoys, something to sit on, plus adequate warm clothing and footwear. If the fowler is competent at calling geese this adds another fascinating and often highly effective dimension. The general principle of decoying is to locate ground where the geese are actually feeding regularly and then to 'set up shop' in the pre-dawn darkness and await the arrival of customers as the day begins to break. There is a good deal of skill involved in setting out the decoys correctly and building a suitable hide in the right position. The ideal situation is to place the hide down-wind of the decoy spread, the incoming geese are then encouraged to approach the decoys by flying directly over the hide thus presenting some sporting shots to the waiting gunners. The decoys are usually commercially made light plastic shells either half-bodied or whole and are life size. A minimum of a dozen must be used to make an effective draw. As geese will always choose to land and take off into the wind this must be borne in mind when setting up.

This sport is not to be despised. It takes experience and fieldcraft to lay out an attractive spread and build an effective hide in the right place at the right time. When using a guide who is a skilled exponent of the goose call the results are often impressive.

As you crouch, cold but expectant, in a well-camouflaged hide, the faint babble of a skein of greys is heard approaching in the dim light of daybreak. Your guide blows a subtle note or two and a response is heard, a two-way chatter develops between caller and approaching geese. The great birds wheel past the hidden fowlers, their wings making a heart-stopping swishing which makes them sound so close. Circling several times, the lead birds finally set their wings and drop their paddles. With a tearing swishing sound they spill the air from their massive pinions, slanting down for the final run in – right over your head. If this does not make your mouth dry and your knees knock then you have no soul!

Some estates which are visited regularly by feeding geese organise occasional 'goose drives'. As it is seldom possible to base a whole day's sport on this activity alone, this novel form of wildfowling is usually offered as part of a shooting package. These packages vary enormously and may include rough or duckshooting and on occasion a goose drive is used to add a little variety to a driven pheasant programme. If the geese are to be driven off a field, guns are placed behind a convenient hedge or stone dyke which is upwind of where the birds are feeding. The keepers will then show themselves and hopefully push the alarmed geese over the waiting ambush, short-lived sport but very exciting as some 2,000 birds clamour overhead. The trick is to keep the head down until precisely the right moment, then to select one bird out of the mass and ignore the rest.

Inland flighting involves trying to place oneself on a flight line used by geese, either coming in to feed or going to roost in the evening on some chosen piece of water. Shooting an inland roost for geese is a controversial activity. When overdone it drives the birds away from the area, often permanently. On certain favoured lochs and reservoirs excessive bags are sometimes made bringing this activity into disrepute. The least harm is done when the guns are very strictly controlled and subject to moderate bag limits with a halt called to all shooting whilst birds are still coming in. Generally a preferable policy for cropping a modest bag of geese from an inland roost is to flight them coming off at dawn. The best plan is to place guns well away from the roost, strategically hidden on the usual flightline. This method causes far less disturbance to the roosting area and if practised in moderation will not drive the birds off the ground.

Ordinary game guns may be used for inland shooting at geese, provided that long shots are not taken and that the shooter attempts to place his shot pattern out in front. To those who are unused to shooting geese their flight is very deceptive. Their wing beats are slower and more ponderous than those of a duck or pigeon but they are in fact usually flying faster. It is always a good plan to hold well in front when taking a shot, even at comparatively short range.

For a 2½ in chambered gun, the Eley Maximum cartridge with its $1\frac{1}{16}$ oz load is a good choice with number 3 or 1 shot size. If a 2¾ in chambered gun is available this will give a little advantage and a wide range of suitable wildfowling loads exist. There is often a temptation among the inexperienced to use some really heavy shot size for geese in the mistaken belief that this will increase the gun's range. Size 1 or 3 shot is most suitable for inland goose shooting.

THE FOWLER'S DUCK

The ubiquitous mallard (*Anas platyrhynchos*) is undoubtedly the mainstay of the inland duck shooter in Scotland and is also of importance to the coastal fowler. This familiar bird is found and breeds successfully almost anywhere where there is some form of water, from lonely Highland lochan to the canal in the centre of Glasgow. As well as frequenting all types of inland water it is also found anywhere around the coast on occasion. There is a considerable resident population which is supplemented in winter by immigrants from Scandinavia, Iceland, northern USSR and north-central Europe, but mainly from Baltic and North Sea countries.

The mallard is one of the first birds to start nesting and in a mild spring may be seen with broods of ducklings as early as April. Like most other wild duck, mallard feed at night and rest during the day. Their day-time resting places are mostly large sheets of water like the big inland lochs, the lower reaches of the major rivers and, in calm weather, the sea. These places all provide safety and freedom from disturbance. They normally move between their resting and feeding grounds at dawn and dusk. This vast movement takes place twice daily all over the country at approximately the same time and provides the fowler with the opportunity to intercept them – a superb form of sport known as duck flighting.

In September, when the young birds of the year are becoming strong on the wing, the main flight of mallard is to the stubble fields, wheat and barley being preferred to oats. They will sometimes flight very early in the evening at this time of year, particularly if they have found a field where the standing grain has been 'laid' by wind and heavy rain. October sees them flighting to a whole range of wet places – marshes, flooded areas, ponds etc. If there is a good acorn harvest they will even feed on the edges of oakwoods. Once the frosts have started to break down potatoes left in the fields after harvesting mallard develop quite a taste for the frosted left-overs and will persistently visit these fields at dusk.

Really severe frost causes them to change their habits as many of their favourite haunts are frost-bound and they are no longer able to gather food. They will then fly to any water that remains open and if the frost holds for any length of time they will spend most of their time on the coast or on rivers and streams.

As the mallard is the mainstay of inland duck shooting, so the widgeon (*Anas penelope*) is the fowler's main quarry around the coast. Although there is a very small native breeding population, the great flocks of this attractive whistling duck seen around the north-east Scottish coast in winter are immigrants from Iceland, Scandinavia and northern USSR.

Widgeon begin to arrive in Scotland in late September and by mid-October large numbers will have built up in the estuaries and around the coast. A further influx occurs when the Baltic freezes over. An important food for these maritime ducks is the saltwater plant *Zostera marina*. This is a succulent seaweed which grows in thin strips in the area between high and low water marks, usually occurring in the sandy mud of estuaries and firths. As this plant has declined in some areas widgeon are increasingly found feeding on grass fields near the coast and grassy river banks. They also occur on some of the major freshwater lochs such as Loch Lomond. They will often flight well under a full moon and this provides the opportunity for some exciting coastal sport.

The teal (*Anas crecca*) is the smallest duck. One of the 'dabbling' duck, ie, it does not dive for its food, it is both a resident in Scotland and a winter immigrant coming from all the same areas as the widgeon. It is not fond of large stretches of open water and prefers the smaller watercourses, particularly where there is some cover for it to conceal itself. It is very fast and agile in flight and 'springing' teal from a weedy ditch offer a difficult shot. It is often seen in company with mallard, particularly on shallow muddy waters where it seeks its principal food of weed seeds.

The pintail (*Anas acuta*) is not often seen by the average duckshooter and is found mainly on the coast. There is a small British breeding population but the bulk of pintail occurring in Scotland are immigrants from Iceland, Scandinavia and northern USSR. It has similar habits to the mallard and favours the same type of diet. The male is easily recognisable as it has a conspicuous long tail. It is sometimes referred to as the sea-pheasant.

The gadwall (*Anas strepera*) is another dabbling duck that is only rarely encountered. It has a small British breeding population which is supplemented by winter visitors from Iceland, Baltic and North Sea countries. It feeds mainly on aquatic plant material and is rather unusual in that it prefers to feed mainly during the day on shallow sheltered lochs, slow-moving rivers and freshwater marshes.

The only other dabbling duck that the Scottish shooter is likely to encounter is the shoveler (*Anas clypeata*). This mainly immigrant bird is unmistakable as even on distant flight its huge shovel-shaped bill is quite distinctive. Not very gregarious it is normally seen singly, in pairs or small groups. It is predominantly a daytime feeder, preferring shallow nutrient-rich fresh and brackish water. It originates from Iceland, Scandinavia and the USSR.

There are three diving duck which are of interest to the wildfowler. The most common of these is the tufted duck (*Aythya fuligula*). This common duck breeds extensively throughout Britain and immigrants from Iceland and north and western Europe swell the winter numbers. It likes the company of its own kind and may be seen in large numbers on a variety of large, shallow nutrient-rich inland waters. It often uses the same water area for feeding and roosting, with its most active feeding times being morning and evening.

The goldeneye (*Bucephala clangula*) is a handsome diving duck which has the unusual habit of nesting in holes in trees and has been encouraged to use nest boxes. It has a small UK breeding population augmented by winter visitors from Scandinavia. It is quite gregarious, feeding mainly by day in small flocks. It makes a characteristic rattling sound in flight and is virtually never seen on land.

The pochard (*Aythya ferina*) is a gregarious bird and large flocks may be seen resting up for the day on big open stretches of freshwater. It feeds mainly at dusk and dawn by diving in rich shallow waters for water plants and seeds. The male is unmistakable with his chestnut head, grey back and almost black upper breast. There is a sparse British breeding stock, but almost all the Scottish winter population are visitors from Scandinavia, eastern Europe and the USSR.

SHOOTING DUCK

The visiting shooter to Scotland may find it difficult to make arrangements for duckshooting on an organised basis. This is largely because duck populations are inclined to be ephemeral which gives the shooting agent a problem in guaranteeing sport. Often duckshooting is included as an extra in a sporting package and is frequently offered together with roughshooting facilities.

The most reliable and productive sport is to be had by utilising flight ponds. These may be natural or man-made small ponds of up to one acre in size. Ideally, they should have ample shallow water of not more than 12 in (30 cm) in depth and be located in a fairly open position. When managed for shooting duck, these flight ponds are fed regularly by scattering grain, usually barley, in the shallow water. Mallard in particular soon discover this bounty and are very fond of utilising these free self-serve cafeterias, flighting to them every evening for a good easy feed. In the process they spread the word and it is not long before very large numbers of duck visit on a regular basis. It is a simple matter to hide a few guns around these ponds and shoot the duck as they flight in at dusk. This system is very open to abuse by greedy gunners, as with heavy feeding large bags of mallard may be taken. It is easy to overshoot, particularly early in the season when the young duck are inexperienced. When managed with restraint, flight pond shooting is a perfectly legitimate and exciting form of sport offering some testing shots as the duck wheel overhead in the half light.

One of the secrets of good management is to cease shooting when duck are still flighting in. This means that they will continue to use the pond regularly if some are allowed to settle for the night in peace. Grain-fed mallard are absolutely delicious on the table and flight pond shooting does have this welcome bonus. With judicious management, in addition to some challenging sport, a pond may provide its owner with a regular supply of very tasty protein throughout the season. Flight ponds also provide valuable nesting and rearing places for the new season's ducklings, particularly if they continue to be fed after the close of the season.

Some estates and shooting agencies offer shooting of reared duck. This is often a very dubious form of sport as reared duck become notoriously tame. These semi-domestic fowl are usually released on to a pond or small lake and this often leads to the farcical situation of beaters vainly trying to persuade over-fat and reluctant mallard to flap even head-high over the waiting guns. Reared duck do provide reasonable shooting when they have been accustomed to flighting out to a system of outlying ponds for their feed, and then they may fly almost as well as their wild relations. Such a system requires skill and careful management and this is not always available.

Some estates have lochs or large ponds which are used by several species of duck as a daytime roost. Where conditions are suitable, a morning flight may be arranged. This is often superb sport as the fowl will come over high and fast and present some thrilling shooting for an hour or so at daybreak. It has the advantage that both dabbling and diving duck will flight to these places at dawn and the bag may include a number of different species. Another form of inland shooting is the type of casual opportunity that sometimes occurs on a roughshooting day when mallard, teal and tufted duck may be sprung from a weedy ditch or riverbank.

Most species of duck may be found frequenting the coast at some time. For several hundred years wildfowling on the coast has been a traditional and fascinating sport that, even these days, is still available in Scotland as a right to be freely exercised by the public. This right of shooting applies solely to that area of the foreshore that lies between the high and low water marks of ordinary spring tides.

Before the advent of some recent legislation such as The Wildlife & Countryside Act 1981, it was legal to shoot a number of different species of wader like curlew and redshank in addition to most of the geese and duck. Now the only wader, apart from woodcock and snipe, which is a legal quarry species is the golden plover (*Pluvialis apricaria*). These delightful black-speckled golden birds have both a resident and migrant population and are usually encountered on the shore in fairly large flocks. These days no serious wildfowler actively seeks to shoot any number of this attractive species. The widgeon is the principal quarry of the shore shooter. Widgeon flighting on the mussel beds under the moon is a legendary part of true wildfowling.

The pursuit of duck on the foreshore is very subject to the movement of tides, state of the moon and time of day. Local knowledge is essential and the stranger must ensure that he does not get trapped by the incoming tide or lose his way in fog. Detailed local knowledge, a compass and a pair of binoculars and a good retriever are essential equipment for the shore shooter.

LOCATIONS AND COSTS

Anyone contemplating a gooseshooting trip to Scotland would be well advised to contact Alan Murray, who is a professional wildfowling guide. Alan has built up an enviable reputation over the years and is probably the most experienced guide in Scotland today.

Alan controls the goose shooting rights to an enormous acreage in Fife, Kinross and Perthshire which encompasses many farms and estates. He is a fund of knowledge on the sport and even when the goose flight has been disappointing he will keep his guests thoroughly entertained by his unique brand of pawky humour. He will supply all necessary equipment and will arrange accommodation and transport as required. Alan manages his goose ground very carefully and will not permit overshooting. He imposes a strict bag limit per gun according to the prevailing conditions. His skill in calling geese is exceptional, he is a veritable Pied Piper of the goose world and can call in geese even when he is standing in a bare open field. A goose flight with Alan Murray is an experience not to be missed. Cost around £57 per day, including VAT.

Contact: Alan Murray Sporting, Talla, 2, Tweedsmuir Court, Balgeddie, Fife, KY6 3QL. Tel: 0592 741461.

Bob Watson, who is based in Perthshire, is a well-respected sporting agent and in addition to a wide and varied sporting programme Bob offers goose and duckshooting of quality. His agency manages the sporting rights on 26 estates and specialises in providing complete packages, catering for the sportsman's every need including accommodation, transport, guides, etc.

Contact: R F Watson, Scottish Sporting Agent, Jubilee Cottage, Fowlis Wester, Perthshire, PH7 3NL. Tel: 0764 83468. Fax: 0764 83475.

Other suppliers of goose and duck shooting which may also be offered as part of a mixed programme:

David Cooke, Cultoquhey House Hotel, By Crieff, Perthshire, PH7 3NE. Tel: 0764 3253.

3121.

R Marsland, Fernie Castle Hotel, Letham, Near Cupar, Fife, KY7 7RU. Tel: 033781 381. Fax: 033781 422.

Powfoot Golf Hotel

Solway wildfowling on the marshes fronting the hotel, with private fowling on a section of the shore and some inland flighting.

Contact: Adam Gribbon, Powfoot Golf Hotel, by Annan, Dumfriesshire, DG12 5PN. Tel: 04617 254.

P Betts, Kirkcowan

Inland flighting over decoys in Wigtownshire. £35 per gun per flight. Also foreshore shooting in Wigtown Bay.

Contact: P Betts, Burnside Cottage, Kirkcowan, Wigtownshire, DG8 0DJ. Tel: 0671 83408.

Westwinds, Annan

Morning and evening goose flights on the foreshore with experienced guide. Inland duck and goose flights when available. Accommodation in a guest house overlooking the Solway Firth.

Contact: J Heath, 11, Queensberry Terrace, Cumbertrees, Annan, Dumfriesshire. Tel: 04617 480.

Solway Sporting

Based at Mabie House Hotel. Guided morning and evening flights with roughshooting on stocked ground between flights. All-in price including full board and shootings – £130 per gun/day.

Contact: Mr and Mrs McKail, Mabie House Hotel, Mabie Forest, Dumfries. Tel: 0387 63188.

John Andrews Sporting

Inland morning flights with experienced guides for pinks and greylags. Strictly limited bags. May be combined with mixed shooting during the day and include an evening duck flight. Angus, Perthshire, Fife, Argyll and East Lothian. All grades of accommodation available.

Contact: John Andrews Sporting, Muirside House, Bellie's Brae, Kirriemuir, Angus, DD8 4EB. Tel: 0575 74350. Fax: 0575 72399.

PINKFEET IN flight. (Roger Tidman)

11 Mixed Shooting

ROUGHSHOOTING

A N INFORMAL DAY'S roughshooting in Scotland can provide a spice and variety that is unequalled in any other form of shooting sport. The term roughshooting covers a diverse range of activities with the gun – from ferreting rabbits on a small lowland farm to walking after grouse and blackgame on a large highland estate.

Roughshooting may be defined as any form of sport where the shooter is himself causing the game to be flushed and where no beaters or formal organisation is involved – as distinct from driven shooting. The quarry may be game, pigeon, rabbit, hare, snipe and inland duck or geese. It is normally undertaken by small parties of guns numbering six or less. When 'walking up' on a typical mixed roughshooting day these guns form a straight line placed about 20 yd (18 m) apart and, strictly maintaining the line, they walk across the ground usually employing dogs to find and flush the game. Safety considerations are most important and the guns must take care not to shoot down the line or fire anywhere near the dogs which are working in front.

Gundogs are extremely important when roughshooting and a well-trained and efficient questing breed will make a vast difference to the amount of game that is found and retrieved. On low ground where there may be rushes, whin bushes, bramble thickets and other thick cover where game may remain hidden, there is nothing to beat a well-trained spaniel. Springer spaniels are the most commonly used type for shooting but a good working Cocker spaniel is a delight and Welsh springers are sometimes seen in use. The job of the spaniel is to quarter the ground in front of the guns in a methodical fashion, staying at all times within shooting range. Spaniels will hunt the heaviest of cover where pheasants and rabbits love to lurk. The dogs will flush the game freely and will retrieve shot game on command – if they are well-trained. Whilst good working springers are a joy to shoot over, an undisciplined spaniel is a nightmare as it may well career about flushing game out of range and running in to grab shot game whether instructed to or not. Some really bad examples sometimes run the risk of being added to the bag!

Several well-trained spaniels will add an extra dimension to roughshooting and they will produce game as if from nowhere. If the shooters are pukka dog men they may not use the spaniels to retrieve at all, but will have labradors or golden retrievers walking to heel which will retrieve shot game on command whilst the spaniels remain 'on drop'. This is a highly efficient and pretty way to shoot and dogs like this will add immeasurably to the pleasure of a day's shooting.

The main quarry on a low ground roughshoot is the pheasant and in some favoured areas partridge may add variety. Both species will usually run into some form of cover when they hear the approaching guns. Turnip and kale fields are favourite places on arable ground. Brown hares, rabbits, snipe, woodcock may all be encountered, whilst a few chance shots at woodpigeon usually present themselves during the course of the day. As game is normally carried by the gun as it is shot, some form of gamebag is needed. The experienced gun will make sure that he happens not to notice or will miss the first large brown hares which cross his path early in the day if there is a deal of ground to cover. The actual shots are likely to be relatively simple in themselves but the unexpectedness of game flushing makes for difficulty. When a large cock pheasant clatters up under one's nose it is usually just at the moment when both feet are embedded in the muddy bottom of an overgrown ditch.

Superb roughshooting may be had in many parts of Scotland on what is known as 'marginal' land. This is the type of ground on the moorland edge where it slopes down to the flatter arable land in the valley bottom. Much of this type of ground will be covered in coarse rushes, whins, gorse and odd patches of heather. It is the type of habitat that will hold virtually all the game species and a covey of hill partridges may be flushed one minute, closely followed by a magnificent blackcock as a rabbit bursts out from underfoot. This type of sport is often the cream of roughshooting.

On the moorland itself, grouse may be shot by walking up with spaniels or, if one is in the really big league, pointers and setters will be employed. In addition to grouse the roughshooter's bag on high ground may be varied by the addition of a few mountain hares. Only the tyro will shoot more than a few!

PIGEON SHOOTING

The woodpigeon (*Columba palumbus*) is a superb sporting bird and is found all over Scotland, the largest numbers occurring on the rich arable land in the central and eastern regions, particularly where there are ample roosting woods nearby. It is an agricultural pest and not favoured by farmers who are usually quite receptive to giving shooting permission to responsible guns. Unfortunately for the pigeon, they make excellent eating and game dealers will pay a reasonable price for them which permits the sportsman to shoot large quantities when they are doing crop damage and to recoup some of his expenditure on cartridges.

The 'doo' or 'cushat' may be shot in two main ways, both of which provide very sporting shooting. Decoying is a deadly method when employed by an expert. Bags of several hundred may be taken by an efficient gun when the birds are really keen to feed on a particular crop. In the early spring pigeons have a great liking for the increasingly widespread oil seed rape fields which later in the year spread their incongruous bright yellow patchwork across the arable valleys. Later in the year they will concentrate on spring-sown wheat and barley, then perhaps choosing clover and fields where there are buttercups. As the grain crops ripen, they will take immediate advantage of any patches that have been flattened by bad weather and will descend on laid fields like a swarm of locusts. This is the time when pigeon shooters become highly popular people.

A dozen or so proprietory decoys will be sufficient to induce the pigeons to flight in to the killing area. As birds are shot they may be added to the spread which will be more effective as it gains recruits. A well-camouflaged hide is a necessity as pigeons are great survivors, partly due to their super-efficient eyesight. A fairly open-bored gun will be the most effective as this is mostly close-range shooting – number 7 shot and 1 oz loads are ideal.

If there is a concentration of pigeons using a particular wood for roosting, flighting them from mid-afternoon until dusk provides very good sport and very testing shooting. The best time of year for this is from January to April, which is very convenient as gameshooting ceases at the end of January. A strong wind is a great advantage for this type of shooting as, in addition to masking the shot, the wind causes the birds to fly a bit lower. On fine still days they are inclined to come to the roosting wood at a great height and then to make a swift vertical descent to the middle of the wood, providing the frustrated shooter with few opportunities. The waiting guns must be very well concealed, and a makeshift hide and camouflaged clothing will make all the difference to the amount of shooting obtained. A hat to shield the shooter's upturned white face is absolutely essential. A normal game gun with light loads and small shot is quite sufficient to deal with roost shooting. As there is no close season for pigeon they provide the shotgunner with very welcome all-year-round sport.

In certain coastal places Scotland provides a unique form of pigeon shooting. Where there is a cliff coastline there may be many overhangs and caves. Within these places dwells that most elusive artful dodger, the rock dove (*Columba livia*), the forerunner of the racing pigeon. Even the top practitioners of shotgun shooting have been humbled by a self-torturing form of sport employed along the north and west coasts.

The would-be slayers of rock doves are taken out in a boat, opposite the entrance to the caves. A .22 rifle is then fired into the cave where it ricochets around the walls. The doves exit like feathered Exocets. As the boat heaves and pitches in the Atlantic swell, the gun that scores even one out of ten can call himself a shooter.

GROUND GAME

The bread and butter quarry for the roughshooter is undoubtedly the rabbit (*Oryctolagus cuniculus*). This species was introduced long ago and has proved to be a highly active coloniser and survivor. It spread originally from the Iberian Peninsula to North Africa and Central Europe and was introduced to Britain with the intention of providing a handy source of fresh meat. It became fashionable for the large estates to have 'warrens' where the coneys (as they were then known) were contained and managed by 'warreners'. Naturally they were not long in escaping from these enclosures and today, despite the continued ravages of that foul French invention myxomatosis, the rabbit thrives throughout the length and breadth of Britain.

Walked up shooting with a shotgun and stalking with a small-bore rifle are common methods of collecting a few 'bunnies'. Another traditional and fascinating form of rabbit pursuit is by the use of ferrets. This form of sport must be confined to the winter months, the non-breeding season, as ferrets which encounter a tasty litter of baby rabbits underground are inclined to lie up in the burrow and to munch their way through the lot.

Having found burrows which appear to contain residents, the ferret is introduced to the hole and it will then work its way through the underground passages seeking a victim. The ferreter always hopes that it will not actually manage to capture a rabbit and that the terrified occupants will flee from the invasion of their homes by this sinewy predator. The usual plan, if sport rather than marketable rabbit carcasses is required, is to station up to three guns within range of the burrow mouths and to attempt to shoot the rapidly exiting bunnies. It is essential that the guns remain silent, otherwise the rabbits will not bolt but will take their chance with the ferret. Fast, accurate shooting is required and, as dust is repeatedly kicked up behind the heels of the flying rabbits, the need to swing well ahead is clearly demonstrated. If sport is a secondary consideration, the ferreter will probably not use a gun but will trap the rabbits in purse nets. These are light bag-shaped nets that are draped over the exit holes and which spring neatly round the unlucky rabbits as they make for the open to avoid the jaws of the eager ferret.

The lowland brown hare (*Lepus capensis*) is much larger and of more brown colouration than the rabbit. Apart from the mating season in early spring when it may be seen in groups behaving like 'mad March hares', it is inclined to be a solitary creature. It prefers open, relatively flat country, especially arable land, although it is fond of making its form – a body-shaped hollow among thick grass or rushes – in deciduous woodland from which it ventures at night to graze the grass pastures or raid the turnip fields.

The brown hare often provides a shot for the roughshooter as it springs from its form on a walking day. For safety reasons, it is not normally shot on driven game shoots, as is also the case with rabbits. Where brown hares are very numerous and in danger of becoming agricultural pests, driven hare shoots may be organised in February and March after gameshooting is finished.

Scotland boasts its own special hare which, appropriately, is quite spectacular. This is the mountain or blue hare (*Lepus timidus*), a beast of the Highlands, which occupies a different territory from its lowland cousin. The mountain hare flourishes on good grouse ground where it is inclined to multiply with prodigious ease and in good breeding years its numbers may increase by thousands. Its largest concentrations occur on ground above 700 ft (213 m) and it will exist from there right up to the highest tops. Severe weather will force it down to lower ground on occasion where it seems to be totally devoid of any road sense, a fact to which the multitude of flattened white carcasses on many a hill road in winter will testify. Like the highland stoat and ptarmigan, the mountain hare attempts to provide itself with the best of camouflage in winter. Around the beginning of November its summer coat of bluish-brown changes gradually to a pristine white. It is then a most handsome animal, being entirely clad in soft white fur with the sole exception of two black tips to its ears. In the current phase of 'greenhouse effect' mild winters this 'changeling' habit does this poor creature few favours. On snowless hills he sticks out like a sore thumb, making life very easy for his main non-human predators, the golden eagle and the hill fox.

The high ground of Perthshire, Angus, Aberdeenshire and Morayshire is where the greatest concentrations are to be found. Their principal food is grass and heather – it is reckoned that three blue hares eat as much as one sheep and therefore they are not great favourites with the hill farmer. If left uncontrolled, their numbers swell enormously and in order to reduce the population to a level compatible with sheep farming and grouse production, severe culls are carried out over the winter and early spring.

In former years, this exercise was normally practised solely by keepers, farmers and shepherds. Due to the growing recognition that the hare cull provided an opportunity for sportsmen, many estates began to offer driven mountain hare shooting on a commercial basis. This is now an established activity and provides challenging shooting at a low cost in the most magnificent highland surroundings.

Teams of up to a dozen guns are spaced along a ridge or somewhere uphill from the ground to be driven. Guns are usually spaced about 75 yd (69 m) apart and will take advantage of any possible cover available. The beating team may start the drive up to a mile away and will bring in a wide expanse of ground. Invariably, a startled hare will run uphill and as the line advances the hares will move in front, sometimes collecting in groups. The shooter's barrels may grow very warm with the repeated shots as hares at full gallop stream through the line. Those who are unused to this sport may easily underestimate the speed of these animals and be inclined to shoot behind. A hill hare going flat out over short heather can travel very fast and a good swing and a fair lead are necessary if it is to be tumbled head over heels. Safety is a paramount consideration. Guns must be certain of the position of their neighbours and ensure that their barrels do not follow a hare that breaks through the line.

Most organised shoots set a limit of around 200 hares per day, although in the days when the shoot was carried out solely for control reasons bags of over 1,000 were often made. Today's white hare shooter has an easy life. No longer does he have to stumble off the hill with a crippling weight of hares on his back; four-wheel drive vehicles and the network of hill roads take away all the hardship.

WOODCOCK

For as long as man has hunted fowl, the woodcock (*Scolopax rusticola*) has been held in high esteem and has long attracted to itself a very special status as a sporting bird. Falconers of old regarded it as a great prize, as it would often give the best of flights, leading the pursuing hawk so high that both were lost to view. Part of its attraction is probably due to its almost mystical aura. It is a 'here today and gone tomorrow' bird. Although there is a small resident breeding population in Scotland, this is augmented considerably by autumn migrants from the Baltic, Scandinavia and western USSR. These winter visitors arrive in late October through to mid-November. Confirmed woodcock addicts rejoice as the first full moon in November draws nigh. Sporting lore has it that this is the traditional time for the major influx of 'cock. The morn following the night of full moon they will sally forth to the favoured coverts with bustling spaniels and a gleam in the eye.

In addition to the uncertainty of its presence, part of the woodcock's appeal is its unpredictable and erratic flight, giving it the reputation of being very difficult to hit. When it is flushed from cover, it zigzags through the trees swooping and diving, presenting both an elusive and hazardous target to the sportsman, trying in vain to lock his barrels on to this long-billed 'will o' the wisp'. So highly prized is the woodcock as a trophy that it sometimes induces dangerous shooting. A gamekeeper from the island of Islay, on reaching the grand old age of 100, was asked if he attributed his long life to the good clear air of the Western Isles.

'Nothing whateffer to do with it, man. It was chust that wheneffer I heard the cry of "woodcock" I threw mysel' flat on the ground!'

The 'cock, as it is affectionately known, is a medium-sized, rounded-wing 'forest-wader' with an exceptionally long straight bill. The plumage is a warm, glowing, chestnut brown on the upper parts, richly marked with buff, brown and black. The under-parts are a gentle mushroom-brown with dark brown barring. The bird has a short, neatly rounded tail with creamy white tips underneath and almost black on the topside. One of its most remarkable physical characteristics is its high domed forehead under which its large glossy black eyes seem almost out of proportion.

Although principally a bird of the deciduous woodlands, woodcock may be found at times almost anywhere there is cover and in the shooting season it has distinct and time-honoured places where habitually it may be found. By day it tucks itself under a favoured bush in warm dry woodland, loving places with scattered rhododendron, scrub oak and bracken clumps. Its favoured daytime roosting places are often advertised by the scattered whitewash splashes of its droppings. Holly bushes are favourite haunts. The bird feeds at night, flighting out at dusk to open marshy areas where it uses its long bill to probe in mud and soft ground for worms, insects and larvae. Resident 'cock have the charming habit in spring and early summer of carrying out an aerial circuit of their territory at dusk. This is

known as a roding flight and attention will be drawn to the bird by the curious high-pitched 'chuntering' sound that it makes continually throughout the flight and which seems to carry a remarkable distance. Woodcock have an unusual ability to lift their chicks between their legs and carry them in flight for at least 100 yd (91 m) or so. A great controversy has raged in the sporting press for about the last 100 years as to whether or not this is true.

Observant people have lived in woodcock country all their lives and have never witnessed a woodcock carrying young. Perhaps understandably, many conclude that this never happens. The author is one of the fortunate people who has clearly seen the phenomenon and knows for certain that it does occur.

There are very few places where a party would set out specifically to shoot woodcock but this desirable bird often makes a very welcome addition to both driven and walked up days on low ground shoots. The gun who drops a woodcock usually likes to have his skill recognised and there is a tradition of wearing the bird's 'pin' feathers in the hat of the successful shot. A stiff pointed feather about 1 in (2.5 cm) long of which there are only two on each bird, they are located on the outside leading edge of the wing, close to the first joint. These feathers have a unique property in their degree of flexibility and were greatly in demand for use as paintbrushes by miniature portrait painters of times past. The makers of Bols liqueur have long offered a special prize to any gun who achieves a verified 'right and left' at woodcock.

The Hebridean islands have long been recognised as places where exceptional stocks of woodcock do occur and where specific shooting days for 'cock are organised. Some estates on Islay are renowned for this sport and special woodcock coverts were planted last century and are still managed as such today. On these special areas the birds are driven and bags of over 150 have been made by a party in one day in the past, with 50 or so being more common. The island of Raasay was also

famous for woodcock and today some estates on the Isle of Lewis still produce some classic driven woodcock days. The shores of Loch Ness, the Kintyre peninsula and the Mull of Galloway are areas where high levels of woodcock may occur.

SNIPE

Although there are three species of snipe that occur in Scotland, only one, the common or full snipe (*Gallinago gallinago*) is of concern as a quarry for the sportsman. The great snipe is almost a rarity and the tiny jack snipe is now on the protected list. Jack snipe are not normally gregarious and seldom occur in the small groups known as 'wisps', as do the common snipe. Jacks are inclined to sit very tight and to spring out of cover almost at the walker's feet, flying only a short distance before pitching into cover again. Great snipe weigh about 6 to 10 oz (170 to 280 g), common snipe about 4 oz (113 g) and jacks only about 2 oz (56 g).

The common snipe looks like a light-coloured pygmy version of the woodcock. Its upper-parts are light golden brown, barred with buff and black stripes on the head and back. Its under-parts are creamy buff with dark brown markings and pale barred flanks. Its bill is exceptionally long and slender, and is used to probe for worms, molluscs and insects in soft wet ground.

Normally resting by day and feeding at night in summer, the common snipe is inclined to make more use of daylight hours for feeding in winter, when it may be found in a wide variety of wetlands or wherever marshy ground occurs. Scotland has a substantial resident population which is subject to some minor migration in winter. These native birds are joined in winter by a large influx of foreign migrants from west USSR, Iceland, Scandinavia and the Baltic. Snipe during the breeding season have an interesting way of displaying to their mate and declaring territorial rights to a nesting area. This display commences with a vertical upward flight followed by a swift swooping descent where the tail feathers are used to produce a remarkable 'drumming' effect. This is an unusual but pleasing sound, very evocative of the lonely wet wilderness.

Snipe sometimes present a shot or two for a roughshooting party when working a piece of marshy ground. The ratio of kills to cartridges on snipe is normally very much in this sporting little bird's favour. It sometimes lies very close and suddenly with a distinctive 'scaip-scaip' cry it springs out on a zigzag course, which may totally confuse even the best of shots. The snipe, despite its diminutive size, is well regarded as a prized quarry of the shotgunner. In favoured areas, where there is a sufficient acreage of marsh and wetland available, specific snipe shoots do take place. In some circumstances it is possible to arrange drives where sometimes the birds will come over the guns at an astonishing height. Such shooting is a severe challenge for even the most accomplished shot. As with the woodcock, the Western Isles produce some outstanding snipe shooting and the Island of Orkney, in the far north, is renowned for its snipe marshes. Out to the west, the island of Islay is also a Mecca for snipe aficionados.

When in the bag, both snipe and woodcock are much sought after. Avid trout fishers use plumage from both to produce popular patterns of flies such as 'woodcock and yellow' and 'snipe and purple'. Both are very desirable table birds. A woodcock will provide a sufficient main course for one person but the tiny snipe is really only in the starter category, unless there are enough to provide 3 or 4 per person. The traditional style of cooking these birds is to roast them sitting on a piece of toast. The toast is designed to catch the juices from the bird as it is cooked. There is always plenty of juice by the use of this method as custom dictates that the birds are not gutted before cooking. *Chacun à son goût!*

LOCATIONS AND COSTS

Sport in Scotland Ltd

All types of mixed shooting in Caithness, Inverness, Morayshire and Perthshire.
Costs (all prices include 15 per cent VAT):
Walked up grouse – £200–£250 per gun/day.
Walked up pheasant – £110–£190 per gun/day.
Walked up mixed – £95–£160 per gun/day.
Walked up white hares – £125 per gun/day.
Driven white hares – £250 per gun/day.

Contact: John Ormiston or Peter Swales, Sport in Scotland Ltd, 22, Market Brae, Inverness, IV2 3AB. Tel: 0463 222757/232104. Telex: 75446.

R F Watson, Scottish Sporting Agent

Pigeon, rabbit, grouse and all types of mixed shooting on 30 estates from Caithness to the Borders.
Costs (exclusive of VAT):
Roughshooting (3 grades) – £50–£150 per gun/day.
Walked up grouse – approx £150 per gun/day.
Grouse over pointers – £100 per gun/day.
   Contact: R F Watson, Scottish Sporting Agent, Jubilee Cottage, Fowlis Wester, Perthshire, PH7 3NL. Tel: 0764 83468. Fax: 0764 83475.

Invery House Hotel

Grouse, pheasant, partridge, pigeon, rabbit and wildfowl on Deeside.
Costs (exclusive of VAT):
Walked up grouse over dogs – £40–£45/brace.
Walked up pheasant – £90 per gun/day.
Walked up partridge – £90 per gun/day.
Pigeon and rabbit – £25 per gun/day.
Duck flight – £35–£50 gun/flight.
Goose flight – £50–£70 gun/flight.
   Contact: Invery House Hotel, Banchory, Royal Deeside, Kincardineshire, AB3 3NJ. Tel: 03302 4712. Telex: 73737. Fax: 03302 4712.

Cultoquhey House Hotel, Perthshire

Walked up grouse, mixed days and driven white hares in Perthshire. Informal, friendly, country house accommodation. Prices on application.
   Contact: David Cooke, Cultoquhey House Hotel, By Crieff, Perthshire, PH7 3NE. Tel: 0764 3253.

East Haugh House Hotel, Perthshire

Specialise in providing a week's varied sporting programme and two or three–day breaks. A typical week's sport might include grouse over pointers, walked up pheasant and mixed game, goose and duck flighting, ferreted rabbits and pigeon decoying. Cost: approx £375 per gun/week plus VAT. Shorter periods approx pro rata. Perthshire and Angus.
   Contact: Neil McGann, East Haugh House Hotel, By Pitlochry, Perthshire, PH16 5JS. Tel: 0796 33121.

Alvie Estate

Both high and low ground roughshooting on the 10,600 acre estate. Self-catering cottages and shooting lodge available. Costs on application.
   Contact: Nick Lewtas, Alvie Estate Office, Kincraig, Kingussie, Inverness-shire, PH21 1NE. Tel: 05404 255/249. Fax: 05404 380.

Fernie Castle Hotel

All types of mixed shooting in Fife.
Costs (excluding VAT):
Partridge/pheasant – £100 per gun/day.
Pigeon/rabbit/duck and goose flights – £40 per gun.
   Contact: Mr R Marsland, Fernie Castle Hotel, Letham, Near Cupar, Fife, KY7 7RU. Tel: 033781 381. Fax: 033781 422.

Alan Murray Sporting

All types of mixed shooting in Fife, Kinross and Perthshire. Costs on application.
   Contact: Alan Murray or Richard Steele,

Alan Murray Sporting, Talla, 2, Tweedsdale Court, Balgeddie, Fife, KY6 3QL. Tel: 0592 741461.

Scone Estates

From early September to November, days of mixed shooting can be organised for parties of seven to nine guns. A combination of walked up and driven, they may be tailored to clients' wishes. Bags of 50 to 150 head of game may include blackgame, partridge, woodcock, snipe, duck, pheasants, pigeons, hares and rabbits. Individual or up to four consecutive days arranged. In February and March driven white hare shooting may be arranged, two consecutive days if required. Bags of up to 400 per day are not uncommon. Perthshire. Costs on application.
   Contact: The Factor, Estates Office, Scone Palace, Perth, PH2 6BD. Tel: 0738 52308. Fax: 0738 52588.

The Kildonan Hotel

Mixed rough shooting on the 6,800 acre Drumlanford Estate in Ayrshire. Prices on application.
   Contact: Iain Bibby, The Kildonan Hotel, Barrhill, Ayrshire. Tel: 0465 82360.

Tulchan Estate

A wide variety of high and low ground game may be shot in the course of a day's mixed shooting on this extensive Speyside estate. Accommodation in historic Tulchan Lodge, a favourite of King Edward VII.
   Contact: Tim Kirkwood, Factor, Tulchan

Estate, Grantown-on-Spey, Morayshire, PH26 3PW. Tel: 08075 200/261.

Tweed Valley Hotel

Mixed shooting including grouse, blackgame, duck, partridge, pheasant, hares and rabbits. Accommodation at the hotel.

Contact: Charles Miller, Tweed Valley Hotel, Walkerburn, EH43 6AA. Tel: 089687 636. Fax: 089687 639.

John Andrews Sporting

All types of mixed shooting for all species for parties of one to ten guns in Perthshire, Angus, Outer Hebrides, Morayshire, Caithness and East Lothian. Driven white hares from November to February. Varied sporting programmes of gameshooting with gamefishing in September and October. The complete sporting service. Guns, tackle, clothing, vehicles, gundogs and handlers provided if required.

Contact: John Andrews Sporting, Muirside House, Bellie's Brae, Kirriemuir, Angus, DD8 4BB. Tel: 0575 74350. Fax: 0575 72399.

Scaliscro Estate

Driven and walked up woodcock shooting and mixed shooting weeks including grouse, snipe, duck and hind stalking from October onwards with prices ranging from £80 plus VAT per gun/day.

Contact: Estates Officer, Scaliscro, Uig, Isle of Lewis, PA86 9EL. Tel: 085175 325. Fax: 085175 393.

A GOOD buck in red summer livery. (*Neil McIntyre*)

12 Red Deer

THE SWITCH

THE GIRL LOPED down the steps of the big advertising agency and paused. She was impressive. Almost six feet tall, long raven-black hair cascaded to her sleek waist, her body doing full justice to the close fitting haute-couture business suit. The green eyes of Tara Fraser were thoughtful. In her mind she was far from the treadmill of soulless London commerce.

What she saw was distance, what she heard was silence. She was sixteen again.

Recalling that well-remembered day, she felt once more the cool northern wind through her hair, her slim legs straining to reach the ridge as her lungs sucked in the pure Sutherland air. She stopped and looked far out across vast space – an empty primitive landscape, mastered by the erupting bulk of Suilven and Canisp. In that sudden moment of her life she knew that this was her land. Argyll MacKay, the stalker, was slightly ahead of her, burdened with anxious concentration. Great was the responsibility which he carried. The laird's niece must shoot her first stag on this her birthday. One of the old school of Highland clan chiefs, Ewan Fraser, Laird of Glenalladale, like to do things in the old style. He himself had shot his first stag on his sixteenth birthday and he badly wanted Tara

to do the same.

She did shoot her stag, an ageing thick-necked ten-pointer. Urgently egged on by MacKay through a long wet excruciating stalk, she got him in the last desperate hour of light, way far out on the march in distant Corrie Glas.

Briefly, a warm smile of reminiscence dwelt on Tara's face. Back through the years she saw again their joint triumph. Anticipation tingled through her, tomorrow she would return. She strode the city pavements into Pall Mall entering the shop of Hardy Bros, purveyor of sporting goods to Her Majesty. There she purchased three pairs of heavy wool stockings and with a spring in her step she made for the multi-storey car park. Spurning the lift, she bounded up the dreary flights of concrete, collected her MGB and headed home to Knightsbridge.

On the Inverness plane next morning Tara thought about her father. Jim Fraser was well-known in the City, in fact the City would say he was notorious, particularly after that hasty exit from Hong Kong and the ill-fated Fraser-Walter project. His devious dealings had nearly earned him a jail sentence and these days the cabinet minister who was his former business partner would not even speak to him. He had amassed a large personal fortune and his life seemed to revolve around adding to it. Her Uncle Ewan, chief of the Clan Fraser, had

a talent in quite another direction. He had fallen heir to the extensive clan territories forming the Glenalladale estates with which he seemed to do little else but lose money. She pondered on how much longer he could keep the ancient clan lands and family estate together. She was familiar with the many problems which beset the estate but she knew nothing of the chief's personal struggle for survival against the creeping malevolence that was destroying the hard, well-seasoned body from inside – one fight that the old commando would never win. On the day that she was twenty-one, swearing her to absolute secrecy, Uncle Ewan had shown her his will. She was to be sole heiress to what was left of the Fraser fortune. Glenalladale was to be hers alone, her uncle being most insistent that his brother should not know of this.

'Jim Fraser,' he vowed, 'may yet win the title but he will never have Glenalladale. White settlers will never invade the lands of this clan and timeshare tycoons will never strip this estate to the bone.'

To Tara's eternal astonishment the estate had managed somehow to remain intact in the years since and her uncle kept rolling on despite some traumatic financial upheavals. One thing which she knew her uncle greatly regretted was that he was now obliged to let a good deal of his stalking and during the season he vacated the castle and went to live in the old gatehouse. From August to November Castle Alladale was occupied by a succession of well-heeled sportsmen from all over the world. They were quite acceptable tenants and all treated the fine old house and the facilities of the estate with respect and consideration, but Tara knew that her uncle resented them and longed for the good old days. Time was when he could play clan chief to the full and have house party after house party, inviting family and friends to share the sport of the estate, rejoicing in his role of benevolent laird.

On a recent visit to London Uncle Ewan sought sympathy at her father's dinner table. He bemoaned the fact that he might have to give in to the blandishments of a hugely rich German industrialist who wished to shoot the finest stag that had ever roamed the hill of Glenalladale. The chief had known of this stag for many years and he and stalker MacKay had watched it develop a finer head every year. Both were convinced that the beast, which returned to the same corrie every year at the rut gathering a huge contingent of hinds, was stamping his quality on the estate's herd and he had been left in peace to procreate for year after year. He had been a 'Royal' many times and last year had been a fourteen pointer. MacKay had seen him far out on the march a few weeks ago and, although still in velvet, it looked as if the beast would make a sixteen pointer this season – a truly remarkable stag for a Sutherland forest. The industrialist had stalked at Glenalladale for the past five seasons. He was an able man and knew his deer. He recognised an outstanding animal when he saw one and had offered the Fraser chieftain enormous sums to be permitted to secure the trophy, knowing that the beast would never produce a better head than it carried this season.

Tara and her father realised the dilemma which faced Uncle Ewan. His memories of Colditz were still strong. His scarred body and lame gait were a legacy from his days as a Colonel in the Lovat Scouts and the Victoria Cross that lay casually in his desk drawer was witness to the fact that his war had not been easy.

'The beast is bound to start going back next year and its such a waste of the best head we have ever had on our hill if we don't shoot him this season. His head's worth a fortune. But, hell, he really does seem to throw super calves.'

The chieftain lamented, staring gloomily into his port:

'I really don't want Dietrich to get him. In the old days one of the family would have the honour, but really he is far too valuable a trophy to give away.'

Tara could read her father well. This ball was firmly in his court and she made a successful mental bet on his next move. To give a public display of family concern, play the white man and flaunt his wealth in one easy gesture was too much for Jim Fraser to resist.

'An end to the problem, you old bugger!' he cried triumphantly, reaching into his pocket. A cheque with lots of zeros on it flashed across the table.

'Let's keep it in the family. Tara gets him!'

Thus, as executioner elect, she found herself on this bright afternoon in late September dropping down into Inverness airport to meet Uncle Ewan with hill boots, heavy sweaters and tweed breeks in her travel bag.

She always enjoyed the traditional seven o'clock alarm call at Castle Alladale. She actually did like the pipes and Argyll MacKay, a man of many parts, played them well. She happily renewed her acquaintance with him after breakfast and joked with him about being a quick change artist. Gone was the full highland regalia of the dawn pibroch and now, clad in ancient tweed suit slung about with battered brass telescope, the stalker was anxious to take the hill.

After she had scored several well-placed shots at the iron stag target with the estate's well-used 7 mm Rigby, Stalker MacKay was satisfied that his young pupil of a decade ago had lost none of her deadly skill. Tara knew she was in for a tough day, the chieftain was a hard man and Argocats were only for softies. In the old way, both stalker and rifle took the hill on foot. Arrangements were made to meet the pony boy far out on the hill in the late afternoon, and even if no stag were shot the Highland pony's saddle must remain empty on the trek home – no easy rides for Glenalladale stalkers. Perhaps the laird was mellowing or possibly he was just over-anxious to give his niece a little advantage but, whatever his motive, the old stalker and the young woman were duly grateful for an unexpected lift up the hill road in the ancient Land-rover.

'That's a grand start we've had, miss,' said Argyll, shouldering the tattered and stained rifle cover which contained the Rigby.

'Don't know what came over him this morning. The old boy must be getting soft,' laughed Tara, striding ably beside him across the heather.

'Weel, the big stag's like to be in Corrie Glas in this wind. Ye'll mind fine where that is, Miss Tara. Its a hell o' a walk even fae here.'

Tara remembered well her sixteenth birthday – the exhausted teenager as black dark fell, fighting back tears of pain and fatigue when last she walked out from Corrie Glas.

'You're bloody right there, Gyllie', she grinned, 'but at least my legs are a bit longer now.'

The stalker flashed her a puckish smile. He had noticed.

As they began the ascent to cross the first ridge, Tara admired the way in which the stalker effortlessly covered the ground. She knew that he would grant no concessions to her city-living state of fitness and that he would take a secret delight in out-walking her if he could. Gyllie always held a strange fascination for her. The stalker had always been his own man and although he had been employed by Uncle Ewan all his life, serving with the chieftain in the Lovat Scouts, never had there been a hint of servility in his make-up. Tara was inclined to regard him almost like a godfather yet was acutely aware that the way in which his keen blue eyes often lingered over her was far from paternal. Although her uncle never displayed familiarity with the stalker in public and always referred to him as 'Mr MacKay', she had come to recognise over

the years that the two men had a bond between them that had steadily grown stronger since their first meeting as young soldiers training in Glenfeshie. She was almost envious of their notorious sessions in the bothy during which much good Glenalladale malt would disappear and their annual carousing trip to Soho was legendary.

Although Argyll MacKay was nearly seventy he could pass for a man in his late fifties. Around six feet, he had a light-boned frame that carried no fat and still moved with an athletic vigour. His ice blue eyes, snow white Zapata moustache and deliberately overlong hair created a maned Viking look, that lent credibility to local folklore that had chronicled his many sirings countrywide from Inverness to Wick. As they walked on, looking closely at him in profile, Tara realised with a start where she had recently seen that same distinctive aquiline nose. A smaller version of it graced the features of the new pony boy.

An hour later they had crossed the first ridge and were three miles into the hill. By now the stalker halted frequently, pulling out the battered brass Ross telescope and carefully spying all the ground in front of them. As they approached the range of hills that folded round Corrie Glas they made two considerable detours, to avoid disturbing groups of hinds with attendant amorous stags that were spread across their direct line into the corrie. A circuitous route was necessary to avoid being seen and also to ensure that they did not come up-wind of the deer.

'If yon big fella is in the corrie, sure as hell he'd likely see the beasts down here scatter

and he'd be away o'er the march in a flash.'

On the climb up to the corrie, as they eased round the side of a knoll, a stag roared nearby. Argyll froze and gradually eased himself down into a prone position gesturing to Tara to do the same. Pulling out the telescope he squirmed up behind a clump of heather and put the glass to his eye.

'Dammit,' he hissed. 'I thought that beast was deid. I haven't seen him for the last two years and here he is humpin' a' thae guid hinds. Take a look at the bastard.'

Tara took the proferred telescope and carefully eased herself up behind the heather clump. Four hundred yards away was a group of around twenty hinds and patrolling round them was a mean and scrawny-looking stag, which stopped occasionally to thrash at the ground with his forefeet and to throw up his head in a throaty roar. He was rangy and long bodied but what made him really unusual was the head that he carried. One antler was of normal shape with a couple of short tines but the other was bizarre. It stuck almost straight out from the forehead, unicorn style, with not a single tine from the coronet to the wickedly sharp point – a deadly weapon of destruction.

The beast was a 'switch' explained the stalker and, apart from being an undesirable type of head from an aesthetic point of view, the single shaft of antler could be used to unfair advantage when fighting. As it had no tines along its length to prevent penetration, the antler could be used spear fashion to wound opponents mortally. This 'switch' was particularly unusual and dangerous as the antler pointed almost straight forward and could easily be driven into another beast. The stalker was concerned that any of this stag's offspring might inherit the same unwelcome characteristics. He shook his fist in the beast's direction.

'That brute killed at least five of my guid young stags twa years ago at the rut an' I never managed to get him. I've nae idea where he disappeared to but he's bloody well back on oor ground noo. I really must get the bastard this time but we just have'nae got time the day. Yon's a right open place where he is and it would take till dark afore we could get intae him in this wind. He's in our bloody road too and the only way round him is to go up the burn. Sorry, miss, but ye'll have tae get your feet wet if we're tae get up to your big stag.'

A hill burn spilled out of Corrie Glas forming a watery staircase down a miniature gorge. By utilising this cover they were able to keep out of sight of the switch and his harem. Argyll grinned wickedly and shrugged his shoulders resignedly when they came to a place where it was necessary to wade up to the knees. Tara tried to look as if she did this every day.

Issuing forth from the narrow entrance to the corrie, the burn spurted over the abrupt edge that fell sharply to the slope beneath, spraying into the narrow gorge up which the stalker and the young woman were laboriously making their way. It was like climbing up a rocky showerbath and with relief Argyll reached the top and gave his hand to Tara, pulling her up beside him. They paused to catch their breath beside the little waterfall.

'I'll just tak a wee spy afore we climb out of here,' Argyll whispered, undoing the leather cover of the Ross. As he heaved himself up out of the gully he did not even get the telescope to his eye. A sharp hissing intake of breath drew Tara's eyes to his face. She had never seen him stuck for words before but now his mouth struggled to speak as he slid back beside her. A frenzied finger jabbed upwards and it took some seconds for the desperate whisper to burst forth.

'Jesus, Miss, he's just up there!'

He scrabbled at the strap of the rifle cover and, withdrawing the 7 mm, swiftly crammed in four rounds and worked one into the breech.

'Quick! Ye'll nail him nae bother.'

A startling deep roar boomed out right above them. Through the gushing of the burn they heard a sudden thudding of hooves, feeling the slight vibration of beasts moving fast. Argyll's face signalled urgency. Thrusting the rifle at her he almost pushed her out of the gully. Tara wriggled over the sheltering edge of the burn. The whole basin of the lower corrie came in view as a sharp musky odour filled her nostrils. Rutting stag stench wafted strongly over her. Not twenty yards distant a great dark stag thrashed with massive antlers at the recumbent form of a reluctant hind. Nearby a group of other hinds fidgeted impatiently and trotted nervously across a nearby knoll. A desperate whisper came at her from below.

'Shoot Tara, shoot for God's sake!'

The beast was magnificent. His body, dripping black from the peat wallow, was strong and vigorous, reeking of virility. The stag's hooves churned a splatter of turf as his antlers prodded the hind to her feet. With a quick heave the stag mounted, thrusting sharply. Finishing swiftly he slid off the hind, a roar of conquest issuing forth from the saliva dripping jaws. In mid roar he turned, looking red-eyed, straight down the muzzle of the Rigby.

Tara had already made up her mind. This was her stag and this was his place. Here must he stay.

Slowly she rose to her feet, staring straight into the beast's face as the roar ceased abruptly. Lowering the barrel, she jacked the cartridge from the chamber. For a second the stag stood, arrogant and unafraid. Tossing his sixteen points haughtily in the air, he gave a snort of disdain and bolted.

She turned, looking down with a mischievous grin at the incredulous face below her.

'Sod it, Gyllie, let's go kill the switch.'

YEAR OF THE DEER

Virtually all wild deer are born in the balmy days of June when highland weather is usually at its most kind. By this time the hinds have been able to recover from the privations of winter and to benefit from the nutritious new grazing of the early summer. Pregnant hinds seek solitude on the high ground to give birth. Their delightful dappled calves weigh around 14 lb (6 kg) at birth. They are able to stand and run almost immediately but prefer to protect themselves by curling up in long grass or heather, where they blend so well with their surroundings that they are impossible to spot from a distance. The hind stays in close attendance and will bravely ward off the occasional foray by hill fox and eagle. Even if a human ventures near the calf's hiding place she will circle around in the vicinity courageously barking her disapproval. The calf grows quickly and by August is capable of following its mother over long distances as the hind groups begin to re-form.

Frequently the hind and calf are accompanied by the offspring of the previous year which, after the birth of the new calf, is known as a follower. These young beasts may stay with the hind and new calf right through to the following spring. Those hinds which have not delivered a calf that season are known as yeld. In times past these were often thought to be barren and reckoned to be the best beasts to shoot during the annual hind cull. It has now been established that it is a fairly rare occurrence for a red deer to be barren and yeld hinds are the beasts most likely to produce the strongest calves in the next year.

Whilst the hinds are taking care of the new increment, the stags are mostly found on higher ground to which they are inclined to retreat over the summer months in order to escape from the hordes of biting insects. Their apparently idyllic lives among the summer hills are fraught with several upleasant drawbacks. All red deer are subject to the unwelcome attentions of some particularly horrific parasites. One of the nastiest of these is the nasal bot fly. This creature has the unpleasant habit of depositing its eggs in the deer's nostrils where they hatch into grubs which

burrow into the membranes of the nasal passages, on occasion causing a miserable death. The wicked warble fly is another charmer which grows as fat white grubs about ½ in (1.2 cm) long under the deer's skin and munches its way out through the skin of the back. Obviously this must cause the beast intense irritation and on occasion they may be seen rubbing themselves on rocks and trees in order to free themselves from their unwelcome guests. The herd's troubles do not end here as most deer collect infestations of evil little ticks known as keds, which attach themselves to the skin and grow fat and bulbous by sucking their host's blood. These little nasties are also quite partial to humans and many a crawl through the heather has resulted in their unwelcome attentions. Liver fluke and lung worm may also infect the deer.

Stags cast their antlers annually from late March into May with the oldest beasts shedding their headgear first. With hundreds of sets of antlers being dropped around the hills it would seem likely that it would not be difficult to come across them. That this does not happen very often is largely due to the fact that, unlikely as it may seem, the deer will chew and swallow the old antler. A great deal of calcium is required as the stag grows his new set of antlers and this is one way in which a ready supply is obtained. Stags will also chew at the bones of an old carcass and have even been known to consume rabbits caught in snares completely. Hill ground does not produce the most nutritious and mineral-rich grazing and stags will take every opportunity to replenish the drain on their bodily reserves

caused by the speedy development of their new antlers. The new growth begins almost immediately after casting, the rapidly emerging new set being covered in a furry brown soft outer skin known as velvet. As well as shedding antlers, the deer also shed their heavy dull brown coats of winter. This moulting process takes place in early June and they are soon to be seen resplendent in their glorious silky red coat of summer.

By August most of the stags will be rid of the velvet from their new fully grown set of antlers and will then be clean. At this time, having had a summer of good grazing, they have reached the pinnacle of condition and achieved the highest body weight of the year. The official season when stags may be shot begins on 1 July, but in practice stalking of stags does not usually start until August. For most of the year stags and hinds do not keep company, mature stags remaining on traditional stag-holding ground and hinds and their followers frequenting different areas. In summer most of the red deer population is inclined to take to higher ground with the stags usually moving out to the highest tops. Around the end of September the stag groups begin to disperse; the rut is approaching. This is the sole period of the year, mainly concentrated on October, when hinds come into season and a mature stag will seek to round up, hold and mate with as many as he is able.

The rut is the most exciting time to be in a deer forest. Stags begin to break out from their summering ground and head for the hind areas which may not have seen a mature male since the previous autumn. Stags now take on an awesome aspect – the glands in their necks swell, the hair appearing longer and forming a distinctive mane. In contrast to their lackadaisical attitude of the lazy summer days they take on a purposeful mien. Some will travel many miles to their chosen rutting ground, often heading for the same area year after year. A master stag trotting at speed towards his favoured rutting ground is something worth seeing. Magnificent, he stands and roars his lust across the hill, inviting a challenge from any rival for the favour of his hinds. Many take on a distinctly black appearance, due to a particular fondness at this time for wallowing in the soft peaty holes which they stir up with feet and antlers into a glorious sticky black ooze. At the height of the rut a rank musky odour emanates from these licentious males. Often the stalker approaching an unseen stag from downwind may find his sense of smell as helpful as his eyesight in locating the whereabouts of his quarry, a very real advantage in woodland.

Once into a hind-holding area, the heaviest and most aggressive stags will endeavour to round up and seduce as many females as they have energy for. They will vigorously force their mastery over their females, going to extreme lengths to defend them from the carnal attention of interlopers. Much posturing and challenging takes place as rival stags attempt to steal away a prize. When a beast of equal size and weight challenges another some fiery encounters may develop into serious battles. The stags may lock antlers, pushing and shoving at each other, striving to force the opponent downhill or broadside on when an antler tine may be raked into the rival's flank or belly. Most of the encounters are just bluff and bluster but the beast to be feared is a heavy-built 'switch'. This is a stag with no tines on one or both antlers, just a single antler branch with one deadly point at the end. If such a beast has a bit of weight behind him and engages seriously with another stag then he has the advantage of readily being able to stab his opponent, often with fatal results. Switches are disliked by deer managers for this reason, together with the fact that their unattractive headgear is thought to be a genetic fault and if allowed to breed it may be passed on to future generations. Another type of stag which is considered undesirable is the 'hummel'. This is a stag which for some reason does not grow antlers at all. Because it never requires to use its bodily resources to produce an annual growth of antler, such beasts are inclined to have an exceptionally high body weight and often use this to advantage during the rut. Deer managers make every effort to dispatch hummels as it is thought that their offspring inherit the antlerless characteristic. It may well be that such beasts could be of value as sires for the deer farming industry.

Powerful master stags breaking out may often be accompanied to the hind ground by one or two younger and lighter squire staggies. These impudent underlings take advantage of the pulling power of their lord. Opportunists, they will disloyally ignore his droit de seigneur, swiftly nipping in to cover a faithless hind or two whilst their liege is occupied elsewhere. Contrary to what had been previously thought, it appears that a stag is likely to implant no more than three or four hinds at any one rut and the services performed by these equerry beasts may well be of significance to the reproductive rate of the herd.

A fit and strong stag may hold his hinds for up to three weeks and during that time he will take little or no food. Finally his energy and sexual appetite dwindle and he will leave the hinds. Passion weary and several stones lighter he will head for his wintering ground, leaving any hinds which may still be in season to be serviced by the inferior hangers-on. By early November the last feeble roar of the rut is heard and the hill falls silent to await the winter.

Given reasonable access to lower ground in time of really severe weather, the red deer will survive the open hill quite happily in conditions that few other creatures could tolerate. They will dig down through even very deep snow to reach the rough grass and heather and will seek shelter and browsing in woodlands if they can. They require only a survival diet to see them through to spring.

The danger point comes at the end of winter when a late, cold wet spring may delay new growth of grazing plants at the time when deer most require good nourishment. The scavengers of the high ground may then have a bonanza as late calves, stags that did not recover from the rut and elderly hinds finally succumb to make feasts for raven, buzzard, eagle, hoodie and hill fox.

The hills of May at last bloom green again and the beasts graze greedily, quickly recovering condition lost to the privations of winter. The hinds are becoming heavy with calf and need the nourishing early bite to provide life-giving milk for the calves which are soon to be born.

MANAGING SCOTLAND'S FINEST WILD ANIMAL

Bison, bear, wolf, wild boar, lynx and reindeer have long since vanished from these islands, mostly exterminated by the greedy hand of man who also destroyed much of their forest habitat. When so many of the large wild mammals that originally roamed the British Isles have disappeared it says a great deal for the tenacity and adaptability of the red deer (*Cervus elaphus*) that not only does it still survive today, but also that its population is increasing at a significant rate and currently numbers around 300,000 in Scotland. Compared to the figure of 180,000 in the 1960s this shows a dramatic increase, despite an annual estimated cull of some 42,000 beasts from the national herd.

The wild hill hind will normally produce her first calf when she is three years old. Often she will miss a year and then bring forth a regular annual addition to the herd from age five to 15 or 16, which is her average life span. The deer herd has no natural predators, apart from an insignificant number of very young calves taken by foxes and golden eagles, other than lack of nutrition and the cruel hand of winter. Thus, even allowing for a common over-winter calf survival rate of only one in three, the annual increment in the overall population is substantial.

As the Scottish red deer population grows so, unfortunately, does its available feeding range diminish. The vast creeping rash of commercial conifers continues its relentless blight of the open Scottish hill. The stark wire fences enclosing the sterile timber factories bar the way to many parts of the beast's high pasture and traditonal wintering grounds. This restriction on the movement of deer causes major problems in some areas, particularly where numbers have been allowed to escalate. Red deer are now beginning to colonise areas where they have never been established before, like some of the grouse moors of Angus. A sad byproduct of overstocked hill ground is that the best and larger stags, which require the most nourishment, will come to seek out more substantial rations and begin to make depredations on the low-ground arable fields, being particularly fond of turnips. They are then extremely vulnerable to the wrath of farmers who are permitted by law to shoot these opportunist raiders as marauders. This is a loophole in the deer protection legislation which unfortunately is frequently abused leading to unselective culling of many prime stags. This policy is extremely wasteful as these are the very beasts needed to stamp their quality on future generations.

'Deer forests', as they are traditionally known, are areas of normally high ground which contain a permanent stock of red deer and are managed to produce the best from the herd in terms of quality beasts, sport and venison production. Some farsighted forests have a policy of providing supplementary feeding during the winter. They find that this

is a boon in encouraging their stags to remain on their ground, safely away from the temptation of turnip fields and eager farmers with an eye for marauders. Beasts receiving this assistance come through the winter in better condition, and in some cases winter feeding may make all the difference between life and death. Such careful husbandry is not solely motivated by humanitarian concerns – no one will pay the estate to shoot a dead stag and, at a going rate of around £250 to shoot the stag and the resulting carcass value of around £100, it is an economically viable proposition to ensure a good stock of healthy stags on the estate for the stalking season.

Stags are easier than hinds to encourage to come to a winter feed, and in a very short time they become exceedingly tame and will come running full tilt to answer the keeper's call which they soon associate with a feed of tasty cattle nuts, hay or turnips. Being able to study the local stags at close quarters is a major advantage for the professional stalker. If there is a tagging policy in operation some of his beasts may be wearing a visible ear tag and he will be able to consult the records to establish exact age and whereabouts of birth, all useful information for management purposes. He will note the inferior beasts that should be culled and will have his eye on several prime quality stags which he will endeavour to keep on his ground to service the resident stock of hinds. Although all these stags will wear a different head come the stalking season, the experienced deer manager will recognise the bulk of them and will often know them so well that he may predict where they are to be found at rutting time. The hinds take longer to adjust to the free hand-outs, but they also benefit and are subsequently in better condition for calving.

If it is a policy of the estate to tag deer, then calving time in June is when this must take place. The stalker needs to be able to track down the whereabouts of the newly born calf within the first week of birth, as even the most athletic are not sufficiently fleet of foot to catch an agile deer calf beyond that age. Finding the calf is a skilled job and the stalker must study his hinds carefully, noting when they give birth and deduce by their movements where the youngster is likely to be hidden. The calves are very difficult to spot and once located must be sneaked up on and secured with a large version of a butterfly net. A plastic tag is then fixed in the calf's ear and noted by number in the estate records. This tag is of a size that may, in later years, be picked out at a distance by a powerful glass and the beast identified for age by a system of colour coding. Thus much accurate and helpful information is collated which assists in determining the overall management policies.

All well-managed deer forests have established an optimum number of stags that may be shot in season without detriment to the overall herd numbers. A corresponding ratio of hinds must also be culled every year in order to ensure that numbers do not become too great for the ground to support. Generally speaking the overall situation regarding deer populations in Scotland is far from perfect. Traditional management policies were inclined to be overlight on the hind cull. It was previously thought that more hinds meant

better stag production and on many estates there is currently a ratio of one stag to around seven hinds. The Red Deer Commission advises that the optimum ratio for a really healthy herd is one stag to 1.5 hinds. There are generally too many deer overall for the available grazing to support on many Scottish forests and a more severe cull of hinds is recommended. Due to the high commercial value of stag stalking some areas have been inclined to take too great a cull of their stag stock. As there is a high demand from sportsmen for the best possible heads, older beasts have been inclined to be over-exploited and there is beginning to be a general shortage of fully mature stags in the five to nine-year age bracket. Unfortunately, this is the class of stag most likely to fall victim out of season as a marauder.

Deer forests and stalking estates derive sufficient income from the lease of stag stalking and the usual situation in Scotland is that demand is inclined to exceed supply for stags during the July to October season. Visiting sportsmen are less interested in hind stalking, which by law is confined to the inhospitable months of November through to February. Therefore the appropriate cull of hinds is most frequently carried out by the resident professional stalker with no sporting revenue accruing to the estate, although virtually all the resultant venison is sold to the game dealer. In many respects, hind stalking presents more of a sporting challenge than the pursuit of stags and an increasing number of enthusiasts are taking advantage of the very reasonable prices charged for this winter sport.

Culling the correct number of hinds is an essential part of managing a stock of red deer. Good deer management requires a totally objective, unsqueamish and unromantic approach. It is no kindness to permit deer numbers to escalate beyond the optimum number that a given piece of ground can support. The alternative to a quick clean death for a few by an efficient high velocity rifle bullet is slow and miserable starvation for many. The professionals are aware of this and make every effort to achieve their target of hinds in the larder before the really severe weather sets in. An early completion of the cull has the added benefit that the carcasses will be heavier and in better condition than those shot late in the season. Selection of the most appropriate hinds to shoot is a highly skilful business. In former years selection was confined mainly to determining which beasts were yeld (those that had no calf of the year). Enlightened stalkers now try to cull the most elderly and sickly hinds, even if they have calves at foot. This involves the rather unpalatable duty of first shooting the calf since it would be cruel in the extreme to leave it to certain death, as it still requires its mother's milk and attention through its first winter. This rather unsavoury but essential part of the herd management process is a factor which repels some potential hind stalkers, in addition to the arduous conditions in which this necessary task is often carried out.

Virtually all deer forests are comprised of acid land at an altitude which would support no other ecologically acceptable and economically viable enterprise. There is no creature other than the native red deer which can thrive on such poor quality land and in such a hostile environment. With skilled and caring management a deer forest will continue to produce a valuable renewable resource of venison and sport, bringing much-needed revenue and employment into many remote Highland communities.

A DAY ON THE HILL

In the stalking season stags do not normally live close to human habitation. Therefore it is often necessary to travel a considerable distance over rough and steep hill ground in order to come to terms with the quarry. This frequently necessitates a prompt start in the morning and the professional stalker will normally want to begin the day and meet his rifle no later than 9 am. In some very remote forests where all access to the hill is solely by foot it may be necessary to make an earlier start. The stalker has to consider not only the problems of guiding his rifle into a stag, but also that once a beast is shot he has to clean it and then ensure that wherever possible the carcass is delivered to the larder that day before darkness falls. Even then his work is not finished as he will normally skin and dress the beast before finishing for the day.

As most commercial stalking is let including the use of lodge accommodation on the estate, the stalker will usually call at the lodge to collect his guest/rifle or it may be that this sportsman is staying in a local hotel. The rifle will ensure that he has with him the all important 'piece' - a light lunch that may be easily carried in the pocket. There is a need to reduce all accessories for the day to an absolute bare minimum that will fit neatly into the pockets of whatever garment is being worn. Deerstalking has no room for luxuries - rucksacks and large bags will earn snorts of disapproval from the stalker, as for part of the time he and the rifle will be trying to crawl flat and invisible through peat bog and heather. It is possible to leave some form of additional sustenance in the vehicle used for transport to the hill and many a flask of tea left in the Land-rover has been worth its weight in gold near the end of an arduous day. Suitable clothing for the stalker is recommended in Chapter 5.

If the guest is using his own rifle, obviously he must ensure that he has it with him and that he has not left the bolt at home securely locked up in a separate place, as so stringently recommended by the police. He must have a supply of suitable ammunition. Ten rounds or so are usually adequate, and these should be carried in a special box or pouch. Soft-point centre-fire cartridges may easily have their points damaged if just slipped into a pocket and the jingling sound as they merrily rub together may be just the thing to save the life of a stag in the final crucial stages of a stalk. Pockets are easily rubbed into holes by sharp pointed objects and the consequences of this could be dire. The rifle is best carried on the hill in a waterproof canvas cover, preferably with a sling. Protective lens covers are a real asset for the rifle telescope as they will save the lenses from rain on a wet day. The stalker will certainly have some form of optical aid with him, and his glass is nearly always a high magnification telescope. The rifle will miss a great deal if he does not also have some assistance to his vision. Using a telescope correctly is a skill which requires practice and binoculars are easier for the amateur. Even the young and fit will find that the use of a suitable walking stick is a great aid on the hill. It also doubles as a steadying rest for telescope or binoculars and an aid to dragging a stag.

Initial transport to part of the lower ground is usually provided, often in a Land-rover. The stalker will always require to establish if the rifle is a competent shot and that the weapon in use is accurate and zeroed in. There is usually an iron stag somewhere convenient and the stalker will insist that both man and rifle are tested for efficiency by firing a few shots at this target.

As is often the case these days, where the stalker does not have an assistant or pony man he may take with him on a trailer towed behind the Land-rover one of the versatile all-terrain vehicles to assist in transporting the stag's carcass off the hill. There are several types of these and one most frequently seen in Scotland is the Argocat which with a bit of care will go almost anywhere, even across water. These amazing eight-wheeled vehicles can carry four adults and they are often used to take stalker and rifle a bit further out on the hill than is possible in a conventional four-wheel drive. A certain amount of pre-planning and inspired guesswork is necessary, as the stalker will try to ensure that he leaves the Argo in a convenient place for him to return to it in order to transport back any stag shot during the day.

On the way to the hill the stalker will have noted the wind direction and may adjust his initial route to the ground accordingly. The scenting power of red deer is remarkable and they use this sense and their acute hearing more than sight to give warning of approaching enemies. Therefore it is essential that the stalking approach is always conducted into the wind and in complete silence. Having gone so far up the hill road in the Land rover, stalker and rifle will possibly take to the Argocat to make their initial approach towards stag holding territory. Every so often the stalker will pause and scan the ground ahead with his telescope, as he may see a shootable stag on the way in and in any case he has no wish to alert the whole area by disturbing groups of hinds.

A Typical Stalk

Thereafter the day's events might well have followed these lines.

Eventually the Argo was left behind and progress made on foot. This involved a climb to higher ground where stags are more likely to be found early in the season and it is easier to approach deer from above than below. The stalker stopped at every rise in the ground, using his glass to establish that the way was clear before showing himself. Two groups of hinds and calves were spotted on the lower ground and avoiding action was taken to prevent disturbing them. Finally, having gained the top of a ridge, a bunch of four stags was seen feeding into the wind about half a mile away.

The stalker took several minutes to study the group through his telescope and then announced that among them was a beautiful Royal, a beast with a head of classic shape and proportion, justifying the traditional description of 'Brow, bey and trey with three on top'. To earn the title of Royal a stag requires to have 12 points, six on each side with the three top points forming a cup shape which custom decrees should be deep enough to hold a dram of whisky. Two of the other stags were young six-pointers and the fourth was an old ten-pointer which the stalker explained was going back. This was a stag that had reached full maturity and was likely both to lose condition and to produce an increasingly inferior head in future years. The stalker explained that this particular beast which he knew well had been a Royal for the last three years and that this was the stag which they would attempt to shoot. The Royal was to be left for stud purposes for a few years yet and the other two beasts were young and had yet to reach their full condition. Both looked promising and healthy with well-shaped antlers and would improve over the next few years, and in the meantime any progeny which they might father was likely to be of similar quality.

The stags were grazing fairly fast along the slope of the ridge. The stalker knew of a deep burn which ran down off the ridge and which he judged by the animals' pace they would cross in half an hour's time. He suggested to the rifle that they hurry along the ridge and slide down into the burn, getting as far down the face as they could without giving the beasts their wind. Once the animals had crossed the burn and continued to feed away upwind they would stalk down the burn using its cover and approach as close as possible. He stressed that they must be quick, as beyond the cover of the burn the slope of the ridge was bare and totally lacking in cover. Once the stags were well out along this face they would be much more difficult to approach. A quick move was essential.

Half running, the two of them headed along the top of the ridge and slithered down the slope into the concealment of the burn, the sound of which helped to mask the noise of their own movement as a dislodged stone or two rattled away. They crawled down the narrow defile for a hundred yards or so until the stalker silently indicated that they should halt. By gestures he indicated that the stags were about to cross over the narrow water course down below them. From behind a large boulder they waited as the beasts crossed the burn and as soon as they were safely out of sight the rifle magazine was loaded and then the weapon was replaced in the cover but with the closing strap left unfastened. In order to keep out of sight it was now necessary for the two of them to step in and out of the burn on the way down and both were soon soaked to the knees. They reached the place where the stags had crossed and the stalker drew the rifle from the cover, working the bolt to cock the action and place a cartridge in the chamber.

Taking a careful look over the bank of the burn, the stalker urgently indicated that they should move forward. Wriggling on their bellies they gained 20 yd in the cover of a peat hag. Side by side now and drawing the .270 from its case, the stalker whispered last minute instructions, ensuring that it was clearly understood which beast was to be shot. The guest took the weapon and eased himself carefully to a solid firing position, sneaking a cautious look over the bank of peat. The ten-pointer was grazing about a 100 yd off but standing with its head facing away so that only its rear was exposed. Whispered advice from his companion caused him to wait until the grazing beast turned exposing the whole side of its body. Settling the rifle tight into his shoulder, the scope reticule was carefully drawn up the inside of the stag's foreleg until it steadied halfway up the beast's chest. A steady squeeze on the trigger, an explosion and the beast jerked forward into a desperate run only to collapse after 50 yd. The other stags raised their heads but did not panic, the Royal trotted about giving a few gruff barks and gradually drifted off with the two younger beasts. The rifle had been reloaded and they remained hidden for a while until the stalker was certain that their quarry would not rise again and the other stags were allowed to take their time in moving nervously away. A sudden appearance could galvanise a wounded stag into flight and it is not easy to be accurate with a hasty shot at a running deer.

After satisfying himself that the stag was completely dead, the stalker bled the animal by sticking his knife into the front of the chest just above the breast bone. He then put pressure on the chest with his foot, pumping out the blood which helped to ensure that the venison would not be tainted. The gralloch

was the next step. The stalker removed all the beast's entrails apart from heart, liver, lungs and kidneys. The rifle was astonished at the quick clean operation and noticed that the stalker's hands bore hardly a trace of blood when he had finished. He had a further surprise when the stalker dipped a finger in the blood of the bullet wound and drew a cross on the rifle's forehead. An age-old tradition, it was his first stag and he had been blooded.

Although in more feudal times the rifle would never be expected to assist in removing the stag to the larder, he gladly helped in dragging the carcass by a rope attached to the stag's head and forefeet. He was grateful for his stick as he was able to emulate the stalker and wrap his end of the drag rope around the middle of the shaft. By tucking the stick across the small of his back and hooking the ends in the crook of each arm he found the task quite effortless. They dragged the stag about half a mile down onto the more accessible lower ground where they later collected it with the Argocat.

Home from the hill, his evening whisky never tasted better.

LOCATIONS AND COSTS

Sport in Scotland Ltd

They have stag stalking available in traditional stag stalking areas to the north and west of Inverness that requires clients to be very fit and able to walk in steep and rugged country. They also have woodland stalking for stags with large trophies where the *modus operandi* is similar to roe stalking. The quality of stags varies enormously. The west coast stags do not have large sets of antlers. Stalking is the most important aspect of this hunting, the terrain is difficult and the scenery majestic. The woodland stags are larger than a lot of stags found in Europe. A very wide range of red deer stalking (stags and hinds) is available including accommodation of all types.

Stags

Season – 1 July–20 October.
Best time – 10 August–20 October.
Usual letting period – one week (five or six days).
Costs – £320 per day and no trophy fees.
Expectation – one stag per day. If an average of more than one stag per day is shot during the hunt then the extra stags are charged at £320 each.

Hinds

Season – 21 October–15 February.
Best time – 21 October–20 December.
Usual letting period – two or more days.

Costs – £110 per day.
Expectation – one or two females per day.

Contact: Sport in Scotland Ltd, 22, Market Brae, Inverness, IV2 3AB. Tel: 0463 222757/ 232104. Telex: 75446.

Strathspey Estates

Some stag stalking is available between late September and 20 October, rents being approx £225 per stag.

Contact: The Factor, Strathspey Estate Office, Grantown-on-Spey, Moray, PH26 3HQ. Tel: 0479 2529. Fax: 0479 3452.

R F Watson, Scottish Sporting Agent

Stag stalking available on a wide variety of ground throughout Scotland. Average price £250 per stag plus VAT.

Contact: R F Watson, Scottish Sporting Agent, Jubilee Cottage, Fowlis Wester, Perthshire, PH7 3NL. Tel: 0764 83468. Fax: 0764 83475.

James Crockart & Son, Blairgowrie

Stag and hind stalking is available in Angus and Perthshire including accommodation in Blairgowrie.

Contact: Robert Jamieson, James Crockart & Son, Allan Street, Blairgowrie, Perthshire, PH10 6AD. Tel: 0250 2056.

Alvie Estate

Stag stalking (35 to 40 stags per year) is available on the estate. Prices are available on application. Lodge and self–catering accommodation.

Contact: Nick Lewtas, Alvie Estate Office, Kincraig, Kingussie, Inverness-shire, PH21 1NE. Tel: 0504 255/249. Fax: 05404 380.

Invery House Hotel

Stag and hind stalking is available for hotel guests in the Deeside area. Stags £250–£350 plus VAT per stag, hinds £150 plus VAT/ rifle/day.

Contact: Stewart Spence, Invery House, Banchory, Royal Deeside, Kincardineshire, AB3 3NJ. Tel: 03302 4782. Telex: 73737. Fax: 03302 4712.

Cultoquhey House Hotel

Stag and hind stalking available to hotel guests in Perthshire. Prices on application.

Contact: David Cooke, Cultoquhey House Hotel, By Crieff, Perthshire, PH7 3NE. Tel: 0764 3253.

Scone Estates

As the hill is principally a grouse moor and is on the southern edge of the red deer range, very few stags are taken each year and these are normally at the end of the season. The best arrangement is for one or two rifles on a two or three-day visit. There are also opportunities for hind shooting. Prices on application.

Contact: The Factor, Estates Office, Scone Palace, Perth, PH2 6BD. Tel: 0738 52308. Fax: 0738 52588.

John Andrews Sporting

Red deer stag and hind stalking in Angus, Perthshire, Caithness, Isle of Mull and Isles of Lewis and Harris. 'MacNabs' arranged. This is a traditional Scottish sporting challenge where a salmon, brace of grouse and a stag are taken by one person in one day. The MacNab attempt may be combined with a week or several days of salmon fishing, grouse and mixed shooting or stalking.

Contact: John Andrews Sporting, Muirside House, Bellie's Brae, Kirriemuir, Angus, DD8 4BB. Tel: 0575 74350. Fax: 0575 72399.

Game International

Red deer stag and hind stalking in Aberdeenshire and neighbouring district. Self catering or country house accommodation available.

Contact: Game International Ltd; The Firs, Mountblairy, Banff, Aberdeenshire, AB4 3XN. Tel: 0888 68618. Fax: 0888 63950.

Scaliscro, Isle of Lewis

Stag stalking on North Eishken Estate. Wild and classic stalking on 3 beats of a 10,000 acre forest. Cost per rifle per day (1 stag) including stalker, ghillie and Argocat: around £250 per day plus VAT.

Contact: Estates Office, Scaliscro, Uig, Isle of Lewis, PA86 9EL. Tel: 085175 325. Fax: 085175 393.

13 The Roe Deer

THE LIFE AND TIMES OF THE ROE

THERE ARE MANY people who have spent much time in the Scottish countryside without having even one fleeting glimpse of that most attractive species, the roe deer (*Capreolus capreolus*). Unlike the well-known red deer which may be readily seen on the open Scottish hill by anyone who has a mind to look for them, roe are elusive will o' the wisp creatures that shun the open light of day. It is a tribute to their skills of concealment that they are able to live in close proximity to man without making their presence known. There are even cases of roe living quite happily in parkland within the boundaries of our major cities. Their choice of habitat may be extremely diverse, and although they have a distinct preference for mixed woodland on the lower marginal ground they may be found in virtually any place that provides some natural cover and some even dwell permanently far out on the open hill, sharing the territory of their larger cousins.

A beast that has roamed the British Isles in a form totally unchanged since Pleistocene times, the roe is one of the longest surviving animals in Britain. Unlike the south of England, where roe became almost extinct in the eighteenth century, Scotland has always had a flourishing population which, like the comparatively recent upsurge in England, is increasing in number and extending its territory. Whilst the heaviest stocks of roe exist in Morayshire, Perthshire, Inverness-shire and Aberdeenshire, they are found in every Scottish county and even the vast empty moorlands of Caithness have been colonised in recent years with a new breed of open country roe.

It is only in the last 25 years or so that roe have been recognised in Scotland as a sporting quarry of real worth. Prior to the upsurge in interest in roe stalking, the animal was treated as vermin and many unsavoury methods were employed by landowners and foresters to destroy it. It is difficult to believe today that, even as recently as 20 years ago, snaring of roe was thought to be quite justifiable. In addition to this barbarity, a commonly accepted method of reducing roe numbers was by the infamous deer drives. This was often an occasion for all and sundry to turn out with a motley collection of shotguns, often loaded merely with bird shot. Many a regrettable slaughter took place thus, and apart from the hideous suffering caused to beasts that escaped carrying charges of inefficient shot, the killing was totally unselective with never a thought for any form of proper management.

Even today the roe is often looked on with disfavour by dyed in the wool foresters. Sadly in years past even our biggest landowner, the Forestry Commission, was not above criticism. The roe management policy in some State forests was quite simple – extermination. Thankfully our publicly owned deer are better treated today. It is certainly true that the growth of some young trees is badly retarded by roe nipping out the leader or thrashing the bark when cleaning velvet, but with caring management ground may yield satisfactory harvests of both trees and roe deer, both now of economic significance.

It took the example of European sportsmen to encourage the British to realise how badly they were treating a very valuable sporting animal. Preferred deutschmarks and francs for stalking facilities provided an extra incentive to the reluctant manager of roe. The influence of the British Deer Society, the Game Conservancy and the British Association for Shooting and Conservation has helped to improve the standard and knowledge of roe management. Training schemes for professional and amateur deer managers and stalkers have been run by these organisations for some years now and these have been of great benefit. Happily, in Scotland today there are many areas where the roe deer is highly valued and conserved accordingly, and the visiting sportsman should have no difficulty in obtaining high quality stalking from a knowledgeable source.

Roe are always smaller at close quarters than they appear to be at a distance. They stand only a little over 2 ft (60 cm) at the shoulder, the bucks weighing 45 to 70 lb (10 to 15 kg) and the does 35 to 55 lb (8 to 12 kg). Their winter coat is a dark mousy brown, long and thick with a very prominent white rump which readily catches the eye as a group take flight through the woods. Their suit of summer is a dramatic change – a silky smooth coat of russet red which causes them to stand out boldly against the bright greens of new summer foliage. A typical mature buck will carry antlers of six points, very rough and with an astonishing variety of shapes. Bucks from a specific area often show similar characteristics in antler shape and style. Unlike red deer they cast their antlers in late autumn, being in velvet for the winter and coming into clean, hard antler by early May.

The roe deer rut takes place at the end of July to early August. It is a less dramatic affair than that of the red deer yet it involves some interesting behaviour. Although when alarmed the bark of the buck is heard on occasion throughout the year, now it rings through the woods more frequently as master bucks drive off rivals. At this time the roe sometimes have a curious ritual. They create roe rings, a circular path worn in the grass by their hooves as the bucks chase the does round and round, usually with a tree stump or a bush in the centre of the circle. These mating grounds are usually formed in clearings among trees and the same place is often used year after year. At this time the bucks may lose a good deal of their normal caution, and it is not unusual for

the dawn stalker to have a doe trot by him with a buck closely sniffing her rear, both quite oblivious to his presence. Bucks may be artfully fooled by the use of specialist calls which imitate the squeak of a doe in heat. Roe-calling was developed as a Continental art and there are few people able to practise it successfully in this country.

Rather unusually, roe does are subject to delayed implantation and their lengthy gestation period means that the young are not born until the following May or June. Roe kids (the correct term) are one of the prettiest of wild creatures and are usually produced as twins. They grow rapidly, quickly losing their dappled coat of infancy and by the autumn they are almost as tall as their mothers.

STALKING ROE

As the roe has a totally different biological calendar from that of the red deer, so is its stalking season at a different time of year. This is a highly convenient arrangement for the sportsman who desires to pursue both. The legal season for roebuck in Scotland is from 1 April to 20 October, but in practice this is normally confined to the months of May to September. The doe season is from 21 October to 31 March and the doe cull is taken at any time within this period.

In order to come to terms with roe bucks with any sort of consistency it is necessary to be on the ground at daybreak. In May this means no later than 5 am, which is often the normal time for a client to meet the professional stalker. A loud, insistent alarm

clock is therefore an essential piece of kit for the roe stalker! The professional will have established on the previous day that the client and his rifle are able to shoot accurately. He will have a reasonable idea where there is likely to be a shootable buck and he will guide the client to a chosen area. On lowland estates this may well be a field or open ground close to some woodland. On a northern estate the stalking ground could be open moorland or hill where a traditional crawling approach may be required.

A slow and silent move is made to the area, ensuring that progress is always up-wind, which often involves considerable detours in order to get round the wind. The stalker will carefully assess any bucks seen by using his binoculars. As most stalks involve taking cull bucks, it is not necessarily the best head seen which is stalked and shot. Cull bucks are animals which have undesirable types of head or are weak, sickly or injured. In order to keep the best breeding blood in the roe herd the undesirables are weeded out and the best left to pass on their quality to future generations. Only when these quality bucks are 'going back', ie past their prime, will the wise deer manager permit them to be shot.

At dawn, the deer will be feeding for most of the time, and as a feeding roebuck usually moves fairly rapidly over the ground a circumventing line of approach is often necessary. Care must be taken to see that there are no other deer on the route which, if disturbed, are likely to bark a warning alarm and send every beast within hearing bounding for cover. The stalker will indicate when they are close enough to the chosen buck for a shot. It is essential that this is not taken unless the animal is broadside on to the rifle in order to ensure the best chance of a clean kill. Assuming that the shot is successful, the carcass is gralloched immediately and removed to a fly-proof larder as soon as possible. It is usual practice for the stalker to deal with the head and for him to present the client with a neatly cleaned and boiled 'frontal' trophy – ie the antlers attached to the front part of the skull bone from just behind the antler pedicles down to and including the nasal bone.

Although stalking in open and lightly wooded country is the most sporting way of coming within range of a shootable buck it is not a practical method in extensive thick woodland where the deer seldom emerge into the open. On ground such as this, a traditional Continental method of assessing and controlling roe numbers is often employed. This is the use of the 'hochstand' or high seat. All types of structures are seen, the principle being to place the stalker on a high vantage point at tree top level from which a wide area of the forest may be viewed. The other advantage is that the stalker's body scent is carried well above the deer and, as they seldom look upwards for danger, they may approach the high seat very close without sensing the presence of man. There are ready-made, self-standing and tree-supported highseats of metal or they may be constructed to a number of different designs out of wood.

Although shooting deer from a high seat does not require a great deal of stalking skill, in many areas it is the only feasible method of control. These structures may also be used as an aid to normal stalking where deer are spotted from them and the final approach is made on the ground.

In order to maintain a correct ratio of does to bucks it is necessary to take a periodic cull of the females. As this has to take place in the winter and there is no trophy at the end of the day, doe stalking is not highly sought after and this task is often fulfilled by the professional keeper or stalker. Some estates do let doe stalking, it provides interesting sport and is a useful way of learning how to approach and assess deer – an ideal and economical introduction for the novice. Doe stalking has the advantage that it may be practised throughout the day. The undergrowth will have died back and the leaf is off the tree, thus permitting greater visibility in deciduous woodland. Although the deer will be more inclined to be on the move in open areas at dawn and dusk they often continue to feed in periods throughout the day and are thus more likely to be visible to the stalker. Still-hunting roe does through the crisp and rustling winter woods is a challenging form of stalking and is not to be despised.

The law, as it relates to Scotland, states three requirements for a rifle that is to be used on roe deer. The bullet weight must be not less than 50 grains and be of an expanding type, the muzzle velocity must be not less than 2,450 ft per second and the muzzle energy be not less than 1,000 foot pounds. This means that certain rifles which are legal for use in Scotland for roe deer are not permitted to be used against red deer in Scotland and may not be legally used against any species of deer in England and Wales. This would apply to several ideal roe rifles chambered for cartridges such as the .222 Remington, the .223 Remington and the .220 Swift. Although suitable legal rifle/cartridge combinations are numerous and there is a wide choice available, one of the most popular compromises for the person who wishes to shoot both roe and red is the versatile .243 Winchester. There is a wide range of bullet weights and loads available in this cartridge and a wide range of rifles in this calibre. Cartridges are readily available throughout Scotland.

LOCATIONS AND COSTS

Well-managed, quality roe stalking is obtainable from the following:

Strathspey Estates

Strathspey Estates cover an area of some 25,000 hectares in Inverness-shire and Moray, including about 9,000 hectares of woodlands. The quality of the roe is being built up by the estate's fully experienced stalkers. About 80–100 bucks and 100–130 does are culled each season. The estate can provide roe buck stalking between 1 May and mid-August and again between late September and 20 October. Staffed accommodation is available for part of the roe season at the estate's own sporting lodge.

The basic charge is £45 plus VAT per outing, with an additional trophy fee being paid depending on the quality of the bucks shot. This could be from £20 plus VAT for a yearling buck to £200 plus VAT or more for a medal buck.

Contact: The Factor, Strathspey Estate Office, Grantown-on-Spey, Moray, PH26 3HQ. Tel: 0479 2529. Fax: 0479 3452.

Scone Estates

A limited amount of roe buck stalking is available on occasion. Some exceptional gold medal heads have been taken off the estate.

Contact: The Factor, Estates Office, Scone Palace, Perth, PH2 6BD. Tel: 0738 52308. Fax: 0738 52588.

Cultoquhey House Hotel

Roe buck and roe doe stalking is available in Perthshire.

Contact: David Cooke, Cultoquhey House Hotel, By Crieff, Perthshire, PH7 3NE. Tel: 0764 3253.

R F Watson, Scottish Sporting Agent

Roe buck stalking on various estates from the Borders to Caithness is available. Costs around £300 per rifle/week (expectation – 3 to 6 bucks) plus additional trophy fees and VAT.

Contact: R F Watson, Scottish Sporting Agent, Jubilee Cottage, Fowlis Wester, Perthshire, PH7 3NL. Tel: 0764 83468. Fax: 0764 83475.

Invery House Hotel

Roe buck and roe doe stalking is available on Deeside.

Costs: Roe buck – £50-£60 per outing plus trophy fee plus VAT.

Roe doe – £50-£60 per outing plus VAT.

Contact: Invery House Hotel, Banchory, Royal Deeside, Kincardineshire, AB3 3NJ. Tel: 03302 4782. Telex: 73737. Fax: 03302 4712.

Alvie Estate

Roe buck stalking is available on Speyside.

Contact: Nick Lewtas, Alvie Estate Office, Kincraig, Kingussie, Inverness-shire, PH21 1NE. Tel: 05404 255/249. Fax: 05404 380.

A FREAK roebuck head, probably caused by damage to the antler when in velvet. (*Sport in Scotland*)

Sport in Scotland Ltd

Roe buck stalking on several estates in Inverness-shire and Aberdeenshire. Accommodation of all types arranged. The company will act as sponsors for foreign nationals to obtain UK Firearms Certificates. Usual letting period – one week for nine outings.
Expectation – three to six bucks in nine outings.
Costs – Around £120 per day for two outings plus trophy fees (inclusive of VAT).
 Contact: Peter Swales or John Ormiston, Sport in Scotland Ltd, 22, Market Brae, Inverness, IV2 3AB. Tel: 0463 222757. Telex: 75446.

Kildonan Hotel

Roe buck stalking is available in south Ayrshire on the 6,800 acre Drumlanford estate to guests staying at the Kildonan Hotel. Prices on application.
 Contact: Iain Bibby, The Kildonan Hotel, Barrhill, Ayrshire. Tel: 0465 82360.

Game International

Roe buck stalking in Aberdeenshire and neighbouring district.
 Contact: Game International Ltd, The Firs, Mountblairy, Banff, Aberdeenshire, AB4 3XN. Tel: 0888 68618. Fax: 0888 63950.

Tulchan Estate

Speyside roebuck stalking on the extensive Tulchan Estate in Morayshire.

Accommodation at Tulchan Lodge.
 Contact: Tim Kirkwood, Factor, Tulchan Estate, Grantown-on-Spey, Morayshire. PH26 3PW. Tel: 08075 200/261.

Tweed Valley Hotel

Buck or doe stalking on foot or from wooded high seats. Stalking instruction and roe deer management courses. Accommodation at the hotel.
 Contact: Charles Miller, Tweed Valley Hotel, Walkerburn, Peeblesshire. EH43 6AA. Tel: 089 687. Fax: 089 687 636.

John Andrews Sporting

Guided roe buck and roe doe stalking on foot or from high seats in Perthshire, Angus, Caithness and East Lothian. Rifle hire and trophy preparation service. Buck stalking may be combined with salmon and trout fishing or with pigeon shooting. Programmes of any duration arranged.
 Contact: John Andrews Sporting, Muirside House, Bellie's Brae, Kirriemuir, Angus, DD8 4EB. Tel: 0575 74350. Fax: 0575 72399.

PUTTING THE final touches to a 'hochstand' or high-seat. (*Sport in Scotland*)

14 Wild Goats, Sika and Fallow Deer

LONGHORNS

GOATS ARE NOT an indigenous species of the British Isles and the populations living wild in Scotland today are in fact feral animals which have escaped from domestication and reverted to their original lifestyle.

The wild ancestor of the domesticated goat is *Capra hircus*, belonging to the same sub-family (*Caprovinae*) as the sheep. It is supposed that the only wild sub-species from which the domestic goats took their origin was *Capra hircus aegagrus* which originally inhabited the mountainous regions of Asia Minor. This seems to be the main origin of the domesticated British goat which has economically supplied the modest needs of peasant farmers and the Scottish crofter for centuries.

Although goats must have escaped from time to time ever since they were domesticated, the major influx to the wild was brought about from the late seventeenth century to 1850. This was the time of the infamous clearances, when the crofting townships of many a highland glen were forced to abandon their traditional clan territory to scratch a meagre living from the bare coastline, and to change their way of life from farmer to fisherman. Many of these original goat owners were shipped off to distant Canada, abandoning much of their possessions and leaving their stock to take to the wild. It is a strange twist of fate that our stocks of Scottish wild goats today were founded as a direct result of the desire of English landlords to saturate the Scottish hill with Sassenach sheep.

The goats established themselves in many areas, favouring steep ground where they could use their agility to retreat to inaccessible rock faces when threatened with danger. The Scottish herds have completely reverted to much of their original appearance. They have long trailing hair which may be completely white, black, mottled brown or grey. Both sexes have horns which, unlike deer antlers, are not cast annually. The females (nannies) have thin horns which do not grow much longer than 6 in (15 cm). The males (billies) may grow huge horns which, in good specimens, develop into most impressive trophies sometimes measuring as much as 36 in (91 cm). Billies may be seen with two different types of horn. One type sweeps backwards in the manner of an ibex and in very old males may touch the back of the goat. The other type curves backwards, then sideways and backwards again which may result in a very dramatic wide spread at the tips.

Wild goats adopt a home territory with master billies often leading the herd. They have extremely good eyesight and a sense of smell as highly developed as that of deer, but they are not too difficult to approach when they have been left to their own devices for some years. However, their numbers do require to be controlled and once shot at they naturally become extremely wary and provide a testing challenge for the stalker. Their eyesight is probably better than that of red deer and they are well used to employing it in their defence, thus making approach extra difficult in open country. It is not just legend that attributes a rank smell to goats. As the stalker approaches up-wind, their presence may be forcibly drawn to his attention long before they become visible!

Wild goats may legally be shot at any time of year although the recommended times for billies are June and August to November. A deer stalking rifle is the suitable weapon. The stalker will receive the horns as a trophy and the skin is often worth having tanned or cured as an attractive rug or wall decoration, although the dreaded smell does seem to linger. If the stalker is extra keen he may wish to utilise the meat. At the very least it might make an interesting talking point for a dinner party, preferably for guests that were not one's best friends!

SIKA

The sika deer (*Cervus nippon nippon*) is an introduced species which now flourishes in certain specific areas. The Japanese sika, as distinct from other Asiatic forms of the species, escaped to the wild from park and zoological collections, but it has also been introduced to some areas specifically for sporting purposes. It is in between the red and roe deer in size, standing 31 to 34 in (79 to 85 cm) at the shoulder. Its coat is reddish brown with white spots in summer and brown without spots in the winter. A mature stag will produce antlers of up to four points on each side and they are inclined to be considerably narrower in spread than the red stag. They have a strange whistling call which may sound very eerie at dusk.

The sika inhabit certain localised woodland areas and seem to survive happily in the sterile spruce plantations. They are to be found mainly in Argyll, Inverness-shire and Sutherland. The stalking season is 1 July to 20 October for stags, the best time being 1 September to 10 October. The hind season is 21 October to 16 February.

Sika are hunted very much like roe as they have much the same lifestyle and occupy very similar ground. Dawn and dusk are the prime times and often the best means of approach is to find a high vantage point, wait until a stag is spotted and then try to stalk it. Their venison is as good as red deer and their antlers make a trophy which is just that bit different.

ROYAL GAME

Kings of old loved to hunt the fallow deer. It was just the right size for pursuing through the vast oak and beech woods of the royal hunting grounds and could be pulled down without too much stramash by the medium-sized breed of hound then in use. Sturdy characters those monarchs of yesteryear – they crashed through the woods on horseback, whooping on their hounds in hot pursuit after the bucks, risking the royal neck but doubtless joyful, for a time, to flee the machinations and intrigues of court life. Not for the peasant these beasts of mediaeval venery – off came the head of any peasant who might be tempted to point the bolt of his crossbow in the direction of the chosen royal quarry.

The introduction to Britain of the fallow deer (*Dama dama*) has been credited to the Romans. However its progress to these islands was contrived, it is known for certain that our wild stocks of fallow must have in their distant ancestry beasts which originated in Western Asia and the Mediterranean region. The royal favouritism shown to the fallow was emulated by lesser notables and the species became a fashionable landscape accessory for the

parklands and policies of the noble country houses and estates. Deer parks became the in thing among the land–owning set and several functioning parks survive to this day. Fallow are capable of clearing quite considerable heights and it was not long ere they broke free of the aristocratic enclosures and settled very happily in the wild.

They are, by nature, denizens of deciduous woodland and are not found on the high open hill. The females and young live in groups whilst the males remain apart except for the late October rutting season, an exciting time when the bucks' amorous grunts echo through the mists of mellow autumn beechwoods.

Most people will be familiar with the appearance of park fallow. They have the beautiful yellow brown, white spotted coats and are fat and heavy animals with distinctive palmated antlers. In really mature specimens the palm is almost as big as a small shovel. The coat of park deer in winter darkens somewhat but remains similar. In the wild herds the general appearance is less picturesque. The coat in winter and summer is fairly dark without obvious spots and the antlers are usually less dramatic with really large palms a rarity. Pure white versions, which are not albinos, occur on occasion in both park deer and in the wild. The fallow has a distinctive tail which often attracts attention as it is white on the underside and shows clearly as the deer take flight. The presence of an animal concealed under trees may be revealed as it vigorously shakes its tail to ward off flies.

The triangle bounded by Dunkeld, Blair

Atholl and Blairgowrie in Perthshire is the home of the largest free-ranging truly wild herd of fallow deer in Europe. This area appears to suit their needs admirably, and despite the fact that there are no physical barriers to prevent them from colonising other nearby areas they seem to restrict their movements to within this triangle. There are other pockets of fallow at places throughout Scotland, one of the most interesting being the herd which occupies the islands of Loch Lomond. Here they may be seen, on occasion, demonstrating their considerable swimming ability as they travel at will from island to island.

The buck season is from 1 August to 30 April with the best time being November to January. The does may be shot legally from 21 October to 16 February with October to December being the prime time. Fallow are reasonably active during the day and may be successfully stalked in woodland at anytime, although they will venture on to open ground more readily at dawn and dusk. Their venison is probably the finest to be had as the beasts usually have access to quality grazing and may put on a thick layer of fat that is seldom seen on red deer.

LOCATIONS AND COSTS

There are few specialists in Scotland with access to these unusual forms of stalking.

Sport in Scotland Ltd

Sport in Scotland have pioneered the fine sporting potential of these species and are able to arrange for a wide variety of interesting stalking. It is even possible to organise a package where all four species of deer in Scotland may be bagged in the course of one week's trip.

Costs (including VAT):
Billy goat – £380 per goat, no trophy fee.
Expectation – one billy per two days.
Sika stag – £132 per day (two outings) plus trophy fees. Expectations – one stag per two outings.
Sika hinds and fallow does – £110 per day.
Expectation – one or two females per day.
Fallow buck – £132 per day (two outings) plus trophy fees. Expectation – one buck per two outings.

Contact: Sport in Scotland Ltd, 22, Market Brae, Inverness, IV2 3AB. Tel: 0463 222757/ 232104. Telex: 75446.

James Crockart & Sons, Blairgowrie

They will supply fallow deerstalking and accommodation in the Blairgowrie area.

Contact: Robert Jamieson, James Crockart & Sons, Allan Street, Blairgowrie, Perthshire, PH10 6AD. Tel: 0250 2056.

Tweed Valley Hotel

Sika deer stalking in the Border Country. Accommodation at the Hotel.

Contact: Charles Miller, Tweed Valley Hotel, Walkerburn, Peeblesshire, EH43 6AA. Tel: 089687 636. Fax: 089687 639.

TWO GRAND old trophy fallow bucks. (*Sport in Scotland*)

15 Shooting Organisations

THE GAME CONSERVANCY

THE MAIN WORK of the Game Conservancy in Scotland is to research the main game species and their habitat thoroughly and to provide solutions to their very real problems. The work is mostly carried out by a team of biologists and ecologists working from the Upland Research Unit in Inverness-shire. Because the Game Conservancy is privately funded through the membership subscriptions of conservationists, shooting folk and people interested in the care of the Scottish countryside and its wildlife, it has always been a very practical organisation.

The Scottish Headquarters is at Newtyle in Perthshire and it is here that the Advisory Service operates. It offers professional advice on all aspects of game, wildfowl, and woodland deer, practical courses on various game conservation subjects, illustrated lectures on a variety of topics, and a technical information service. There is also a network of regional groups throughout Scotland which organise social and fund raising events.

An interesting facility which is available to members is the wide variety of training and educational courses which are offered annually by the Conservancy. Their residential courses are most popular and are run for keepers, amateur, professional and prospective, and for people who have recently taken up shooting. Residential courses draw on the comprehensive facilities and experience of the Conservancy's staff at its headquarters at Fordingbridge, while some specialised subjects are covered by external experts in their own field. Emphasis is placed on the practical applications of game management and shooting principles. Time is divided between lectures, practical demonstrations and practical work with outside activities being given a high priority. The courses are open to all over the age of 14.

Residential courses planned during 1991, which are from three to seven days duration, are a gamekeepers' training course, gamekeepers' refresher course, young shots course, and a part-time keepers' course. One day non-residential game management courses cover making the best of farm woodlands, pheasants, farm woods, forestry and fowling, mixed cornish shooting, a Lincolnshire wold shoot with set-aside, shooting on a shoestring, Wild partridges and modern farming, developing a successful small DIY shoot, planning for wild pheasants and partridge, and a game management day at Fordingbridge.

Further information on the organisation and full details of courses are available from the UK headquarters at The Game Conservancy, Fordingbridge, Hants, SP6 1EF. Tel: 0425 52381. Enquiries concerning Scottish matters and details of the shoot consultancy service in Scotland should be directed to Ian McCall, Regional Director Scotland, The Game Conservancy, Scottish HQ, Henderston, Newtyle, Perthshire, PH12 8UT. Tel: 08285 543.

The Game Conservancy has run a very successful game fair in recent years which has become a regular annual event in early July. This is held in the grounds of Scone Palace, adjacent to the river Tay on the outskirts of Perth. Details from the Scottish Office.

THE BRITISH ASSOCIATION FOR SHOOTING AND CONSERVATION

BASC was founded in 1908, originally named as the Wildfowlers' Association of Great Britain and Ireland. Since that time it has vigorously developed as the largest organisation representing the interests of all shooting people. The association has branches and affiliated clubs throughout the UK, and operates a multitude of activities designed to promote and develop the cause of sporting shooting and wildlife conservation.

The Association runs a number of training courses and special events for members as well as promoting game fairs in Perthshire and Inverness-shire. A quarterly magazine is produced for members. Useful information and membership details can be obtained from

The British Association for Shooting and Conservation, Scottish Office, Croft Cottage, Trochry, By Dunkeld, Perthshire. Tel: 03503 226. Fax: 03503 227.

THE BRITISH DEER SOCIETY

The British Deer Society has branches throughout the UK, and is devoted to the conservation and good management of all British deer species. Educational training courses and study days are organised for professional and amateur stalkers. Further information and membership details are available from The British Deer Society, Church Farm, Lower Basildon, Reading, Berkshire, RG8 9NH. Tel: 07357 4094.

THE BRITISH FIELD SPORTS SOCIETY

The Society promotes and represents the interests of all forms of field sports, providing an overall representation for shooting, stalking, fishing, fox and stag hunting, falconry and coursing. It is the most political of all the sporting organisations and maintains a close watching brief on all matters of proposed legislation that might affect the legitimate interests of its members. The Society is particularly concerned about the effects of EEC legislation on British sport. There are branches throughout the UK. Further information can be obtained from The British Field Sports Society, 59, Kennington Road, London, SE1 7PZ. Tel: 071 928 4742.

DIARMID ANDREWS, with a fine eleven-pointer from the Isle of Mull. (*John Andrews*)

Index